MONTCALM COMMUNITY COLLEGE

MONTCALM
COMMUNITY COLLEGE

— Creating Futures Then, Now, Always —

COMPILED BY GARY L. HAUCK

MONTCALM COMMUNITY COLLEGE

CREATING FUTURES THEN, NOW, ALWAYS

iUniverse books may be ordered through booksellers or by contacting:

iUniverse
1663 Liberty Drive
Bloomington, IN 47403
www.iuniverse.com
1-800-Authors (1-800-288-4677)

ISBN: 978-1-4917-7829-6 (sc)
ISBN: 978-1-4917-7830-2 (hc)
ISBN: 978-1-4917-7831-9 (e)

Library of Congress Control Number: 2015916669

Print information available on the last page.

iUniverse rev. date: 12/07/2015

Dedicated to:

All past and present members of the MCC family and supporting community – whose vision, dedication and faithful service helped to make Montcalm Community College what it is today.

Contents

Notable Events in the Growth and Development of MCC

1963 – Feasibility study launched

1964 – Resolution passed to initiate college

1965 (March 2) – Public vote passed

1965 (June 3) – Dr. Donald Fink hired as the first president

1965 (September) – Anderson Farm site chosen for campus

1966 (May) – First applications accepted

1966 (fall) – Classes began in various locations

1967 (fall) – Campus opened with initial buildings (dedication on Sept. 26)

1968 (May 22) – First campus commencement celebrated

1969 – Centurions basketball team established

1970 – MCC baseball team established

1970 – MCC golf team established

1971 – Dr. Clifford Bedore became the second president

1975-1976 – Activities Building constructed

1976 – Pool opened

1978 – Dr. Herbert Stoutenburg became the third president

1981 – Montcalm Community College Foundation established

1982 – First computers installed

1982 – Santa's Super Sunday began

1984 – Dr. Donald Burns became the fourth president

1984 – Nature trails construction approved by the board

1986 – Crystal the Montcalm Mastodon discovered

1986 – Heritage Village established

1987 – Greenville learning center launched

1988 – Crystal the mastodon came to MCC's Sidney campus

1989 – Ionia Educational Center established

1996 – New millage passed (fiscal turning point)

1999 – Beatrice E. Doser Building constructed

1999 – Panhandle Area Center launched in Howard City

2000-2001 – Michigan Technology and Education Center (M-TEC) constructed

2007 – Ash Building dedicated on Sidney campus

2009 – Robert Ferrentino became the fifth president

2013 – Bill Braman Family Center for Education opened on the Greenville campus

2014-2015 – MCC celebrated its 50th anniversary

MCC's 50th Anniversary Celebration "50 Formation"
[Photo by Cory Smith]

In alphabetical order:
Don Adkison, Debra Alexander, Katie Arwood, Lora Bacon, Angie Benn, Cheryl Bergeron, Caron Bianchi, Bill Bishop, Joel Brouwer, James Brown, Brandy Bunting, Karen Buskirk, Jody Butler, Karen Carbonelli, Mel Christensen, Chuck Clise, Joseph Codling, Lisa Cogswell, Dana Cunningham, Darcella Daws, Ken DeLong, Linda DeVries, Kristen Diehl, Amy Eady, Kevin Evoy, Bob Ferrentino, Heather Fierke, Marge Forist, Lisa Gardner, Evelyn Garvey, George Germain, Michelle Gibson, Jessica Gilberston, Randall Gilbert, Pam Grice, Shelia Hansen, Ann Hansen, Susan Hatto, Gary Hauck (Centurion), Lisa Haverdink, Tammy Headworth, Lisa Herald, Jessica Herrick, Pat Hinrichs, Kim Holt, Jamie Hopkins, Sharon Houghton, Serena Houseman, Ginger Imhoff, Amber Jaramillo, Rachel Johansen, Carolyn Johnson, Krysti Jolley, Daniel Jones, Sam Jurden, Joyce Kitchenmaster, David Kohn, Joe Lake, Jim Lantz, Karen Lincoln, Mary Ellen Lingeman, Breanna Lintemuth, Brianne Lodholtz, Kathie Lofts, Dan Long, Lisa Lund, Samantha Mack, Katelyn Main, Beth Markham, Pat Marston, Bob

Marston, Karen Maxfield, Mary Jo McCully, Sharon Miller, Sally Morais, Larry Moss, Sue Moss, Beth Mowatt, Traci Nichols, Rod Nutt, Glennes Page, Al Palmer, Shirley Palmer, Jim Peacock, Doug Reinsmith, Heather Richards, Doreen Richmond, Ruth Rittersdorf, Jan Roy, Billie Sanders, Michael Seaman, Kelsey Shattuck, Gary Shilling, Tore Skogseth, Greta Skogseth, Scott Smith, Terry Smith, Dan Snook, Judi Snyder, Jessica Snyder, Rob Spohr, Shelly Springborn, Lois Springsteen, Chris Stander, Connie Stewart, Julie Stockwell, Glenda Stout, Marquitta Stubblefield, Roger Thelen, Dolores Thompson, Shannon Tripp, Val Vander Mark, Vicky Wagner, JoAnn Walden, Heather Wesp, Kire Wierda, Anne Wiggers, Mike Williams, Ryan Wilson, Amber Zimmerman

Preface

Many refer to Montcalm Community College as the "Pearl of Montcalm County." Those of us who study and work here would most certainly agree. And as we entered the year 2015, we enthusiastically celebrated a half-century of service and growth. With the vote of the people on November 4, 2014, to renew the college operating millage, which provides about $2.5 million annually, the community stood with us in affirmation of MCC's commitment to creating brighter futures.

But the college did not rest on its laurels. In a communique to faculty and staff, President Bob Ferrentino unveiled four areas of focus for 2015:

1. Continuous Quality Improvement – measuring effectiveness
2. Integration of Services – providing more non-academic services to students who need those services
3. One MCC College-Wide Customer Service System – using data to more effectively support students' successful achievement of their goals
4. Helping Students Learn – facilitating success

The work goes on. Yet, it is time to celebrate! Throughout the 2014-2015 academic year and fall semester of 2015, an appointed 50th Anniversary Celebration Committee has collaborated on meaningful ways to focus on MCC's rich history and heritage, and give appropriate festive homage. One of those ways was the creation of this commemorative overview, which, it is hoped, highlights the college's legacy while providing a meaningful record for future generations of the MCC community.

Obviously, any project such as this raises the two-fold challenge of selection and arrangement. Of the myriads of newspaper articles, letters, photos, conversations, memories, and communiques of significant people and events, choices must be made of what to include and not include. At the same time, a decision must be made as to how to logically or chronologically present those items selected, or what to do with incomplete or missing files or information. This being the case, I humbly apologize in advance for any significant work that may have gone unreported, names that we may have failed to adequately recognize, directory information that may be inaccurate, or events that may have been slighted. Our attempt has been a sincere one to request information, interview as many individuals as possible, and include a combination of historical facts along with personal stories.

Acknowledgements

I would like to personally thank Bonnie Schlosser, Evelyn Garvey, and Karen Maxfield for their assistance in research and the retrieving and scanning of historical photographs. Kelsey Shattuck and Jody Butler were of inestimable help in the conversion of photos into publishable pictures and collages. Shelly Springborn and Samantha Mack provided alumni stories and several pieces of information regarding faculty and staff, and Terry Smith, along with Lisa Herald, supplied significant input on the MCC Foundation, emeriti, and distinguished service awards. Board minutes and summaries provided by Terry Smith and Les Morford were a goldmine of factual data. Assistance was also provided by Katie Arwood and Lisa Johnson, and the history of MCC's music program was synthesized by Valerie Vander Mark. Evelyn Garvey also painstakingly created a list of the college faculty and staff by going through 50 years of college catalogs.

In addition to several current and retired faculty and staff members who shared their thoughts by email or conversation, a special word of thanks goes to each one who willingly participated in formal, video-recorded interviews ranging in length from 30 to 90 minutes. Not only has information from those interviews been included in this account, but they have also been featured online in a monthly portal labeled MCC Historical Reflections. These have been included in the new time capsule sealed on November 8, 2015, and to be opened in 2040, during the school's 75th anniversary year. Those interviewed on video were: Bob Ferrentino, Don Burns, Les Morford, James Lantz, Bill Seiter, Ken Smith, Jesse Fox, Dennis Mulder, Bev Gates, Karen Carbonelli, Ken

DeLong, Terry Smith, Bill Braman, Dan Snook, Sally Morais, Jody Butler, and Lois Springsteen. Our information technology staff assisted with the video recordings, and especially helpful were Kyle Shattuck, Betty-Jane Leeuw, Tony Kosal, Daniel Jones, Rick Temple, and Lori Cook.

Finally, I owe a debt of gratitude to Shelly Springborn, Terry Smith, Jody Butler, Bob Ferrentino, Don Burns, Karen Maxfield, and my wife, Lois Hauck, for laboring through the initial manuscript with their thoughtful corrections, recommendations, and refinement suggestions. I will also note that in matters of style, a combination of basic MLA format and general rules of journalism were used, with an attempt toward some measure of consistency.

To all our faculty, staff members, students, emeriti, alumni, and friends of MCC, we salute you for making Montcalm Community College the Pearl that it is!

Gary L. Hauck

November 10, 2015

The Anderson Farm and future site of MCC
as it looked in 1965 and 1966

Chapter 1

————◆•◆•◆————

A Dream Comes True

At first, the thought of a community college in Montcalm County was simply that – an idea, vision, or dream. Neighboring Ionia County had a similar thought, but when taken to the people for a vote, the proposal failed, not just once, but twice. The tiny band of leaders and some of the community members of Montcalm County seemed determined to bring reality out of their ideas.

During the 1960s, the law allowed a prospective public institution to levy a county tax in order to provide the necessary finances for its founding and development. It would be determined by public, majority vote. This was the kind of election that was defeated in Ionia County.

Feasibility Study

A feasibility study was initiated in 1963 by the Montcalm Area Intermediate School District (MAISD) Board, and completed in June of 1964. Dr. William Seiter, MAISD Superintendent, facilitated the initial groundwork. The steering committee was comprised of: Charles Simon, Chairman (Edmore); Phil Peasley, Vice Chairman (Vestaburg); Dee Cook, Secretary (Greenville); and Seiter (Stanton). Under the direction of Dr. Max S. Smith of the Office of Community College Cooperation at Michigan State University, a final report was compiled and printed by Simon.

Following the completion of the study, the Montcalm County Community College Publicity Committee was established to promote the idea of a college, with Dr. Harold Steele of Greenville serving as the first chairperson. Public information meetings were conducted throughout the county, and articles were submitted to every Montcalm-area newspaper. Chairpeople were selected from each area of the county to spearhead the publicity and flow of information. They included: Carol Watts (Belvidere), Dr. Frank Carter and Ron Barnes (Carson City), Herluf Jensen (Cedar Lake), Lee Hansen (Coral-Trufant), Ed McGrath (Crystal), Garrett Verplanck and Phil Daab (Edmore), Roy Burghart (Greenville), Bernice Bennett and Wallace Petersen (Lakeview), David Byers and Suzanne Beardless (Sheridan), Donald Peterson (Sidney), Charlotte Miel (Stanton), Lucille Nowlin (Tri County), and Elizabeth Lester (Vestaburg).

The Publicity Committee of the MAISD School Board met with the chairpeople on Thursday evening October 8, 1964, at the courthouse in Stanton. Members approved the preparation of a slide presentation on the Montcalm County Community College Study, which would become available to any group or organization after November 10. Attending the meeting were Victor Harrison, Beatrice Doser and Simon.

Another meeting was held October 20 at Marlview Lanes near Edmore with co-chairpeople of the Edmore Citizens for Community College organization, Daab and Verplanck presiding. Others participating included Chairpersons Lester and Watts of Six Lakes). According to *The Daily News* on October 22, 1964:

> They noted that the finance section of the community college study recommended a levy of not more than one mill against state equalized valuation to partially finance the community college. They said that one mill would cost the average taxpayer $5 or $6 per year depending upon the assessed valuation of the property.
>
> A portion of the tax revenue would be used to pay for less than one-third of the operating expenses of the proposed college. Tuition and fees of about $200 per year per student would pay approximately one-third

and the remainder would come from state and federal funds and gifts.

An estimated 80 percent of the operating fund would be personnel. The balance of the millage would be used along with state matching funds and federal aid to provide facilities for the college.

On October 29, it was announced that Doser replaced Steele as Publicity Committee Chair, upon his appointment to the MAISD Board. Doser accepted her new assignment with enthusiasm, and led the committee in the promotion of the slide presentation and the calling of several public forums. She also helped to prepare articles for several newspapers throughout the county. One of those articles used some gentle persuasion:

> If only 200 students leave the Montcalm area to attend college elsewhere, they take with them $400,000 annually that could be spent here. Salaries for community college personnel to accommodate 200 students would run about $88,000 – most of which would probably remain in the county. And 200 students could have been expected to enroll at a community college in Montcalm County in the fall of 1964 had one existed. (Doser, 1963)

On November 4, three groups advocating for the launch of a community college in Montcalm County met at Central Montcalm High School and invited the community to attend with any questions to be answered. By November 23, the slide presentation was completed and its first showing was at the Crystal Lions Club, with members of the Carson City Lions Club also invited. A meeting between the community college area chairpeople and the Public Information Committee of the MAISD Board was conducted at Greenville High School on December 9. The results of the study were presented, and the slide presentation was again shown.

Publicity Chair Doser announced that she received at least 36 requests from clubs and organizations to view the slide show. Support for the prospective institution grew, and on December 17, the following resolution was passed by the Central Montcalm Board of Education:

> Motion made by Hudson, supported by Miel, that the following resolution be adopted by the Board, to express public support of the proposed Community College.
> WHEREAS, it is believed that a Community College in the Montcalm Area Intermediate School District would provide increased opportunities for training beyond high school for youth in the Montcalm area, and
> WHEREAS, it is believed that this training would be obtained more economically for individual students
> THEREFORE, be it resolved that the Central Montcalm Board of Education unanimously gives its support to the establishment of a Community College in the Montcalm Area Intermediate School District.
> Yeas 6, nay 0, motion carried.
> Respectfully submitted, Beryl Gavitt, Secretary

In January 1965, the MAISD Board set March 2 as the public election date for the establishment of a community college, and before the end of February, 16 candidates filed for positions on the college Board of Trustees, should the voters approve the establishment of a community college.

Seiter recalls, "Things were progressing nicely, but there was already a concern as to where the new college would be located. In an effort to prevent this from being a distraction during the election, the MAISD recommended a location 'as near the geographic and population center of the county as possible.' This seemed to quiet things down" (Seiter, 2013).

Public Vote Passes – MCC is Born

On March 2, 1965, county voters approved the establishment of a community college and the levy of one mill for operation by a vote of almost 2:1 (3,840 yes to 2,058 no), and as a result, a new college was born. Initial board members elected were Grace Greenhoe of Carson City, Steele of Greenville, Doser of Edmore, Stanley Ash of Greenville, Joseph Cook of Lakeview, and James Crosby of Greenville. On the same night as the election, and less than 30 minutes after the millage was passed, Leslie Morford, a teacher at Greenville High School, became the first applicant to be a member of the faculty.

"When the polls had closed at 8 p.m., it was announced that the millage had passed. By 8:30 p.m., I had my application filled out and ready to submit to the new Board of Trustees" (Morford, 2012).

However, the board created a policy that the new college would not hire teachers from area high schools. But the policy was short lived and quickly overturned. Morford became one of the first hires and taught part time for the first academic year. He was appointed to the full-time faculty during the school's second year. All faculty members were part-time during MCC's first year.

Since the new college did not have an official name, the board held a contest to solicit suggestions. One submission, though probably not a serious one, was Spud Tech because of the potato crops in Montcalm County and farm suppliers for the national potato chip industry. Other suggestions included George Romney Community College, to recognize then-Governor George Romney, who was supportive of the establishment of community colleges: Spudale Community College; Gibson-Ore-Ida Community College; and Fertile Acres Community College, because of the agricultural nature of the community. Ninety suggestions were submitted. The winning name, Montcalm Community College, was entered by Dorothea Krampe of Coral, Earl Eshelman of Crystal and David Pritchard of Stanton. It became official in April 1965.

Because it would take time for the new institution to receive the revenue, Board Chairperson Ash and his business partner, Charles Randall, each gave the college a gift of $2,000 to jump-start the launch of the school and pay the earliest bills. The board also received numerous applications for administrative positions, instructors, custodians, and potential students.

First President

In June 1965, Dr. Donald Fink was selected as the first president of MCC by a vote of 4 to 2. Interestingly, Fink at the time was a professor in the graduate counseling program at Michigan State University, and was serving as the dean of Grand Rapids Junior College. One of his MSU students in 1965 was a young man named Don Burns, who later would serve as MCC's fourth president. Burns did not know Fink was in the process of being hired as the first president of MCC. He had to deliver his final homework assignment to Fink at Franklin Street in Greenville, and didn't understand why Fink was in Greenville. Fink would later leave MCC in June of 1971, and Burns arrived in August of that same year as a member of the counseling staff. According to Burns, "Don Fink moved the college from nothing to something. He facilitated the selection of the campus location, developed the initial facilities, hired faculty, and developed the school's first curriculum, serving those crucial start-up years of 1965 to 1971" (Burns). When Burns arrived on campus, there was an administration building, a one-story classroom building (Instruction West), a two-story classroom building (Instruction East), and a vocational-technical building (Instruction North). "There were still no paved parking lots, but Dr. Fink developed a significant campus under his leadership. He took the concept of the college and moved it forward" (Burns).

Fink held an EdD degree in counseling and educational leadership. Following his service with the United States Army during World War II, he began his career as a junior and senior high school vocal music teacher. It was while he was the dean at GRJC and teaching once a week for MSU that MCC trustees Steele and Ash pursued him as a candidate for MCC's first president. According to Fink, they were "adamant" about him coming to Sidney. Fink said, "This was the one place I thought I would never come to," but he was beginning to feel restless at GRJC and decided it was time for a change (Terence Smith). He later referred to MCC as "the miracle on Sidney Road" (Terence Smith).

But Fink faced many challenges. Not everyone in the community was in favor of his hiring, and two of the board members voted against his appointment. Nevertheless, he was officially hired on June 23, 1965. He soon learned that while the tax levy passed, eight of the 26 precincts in Montcalm County voted against it, and were slow to accept the new reality. He also learned that few students came from Greenville during the first several years, and there was some disappointment in that part of the county regarding the location the school would soon occupy. Prior to Fink's appointment, the board had hired Cliff Bedore as business manager, a title that soon was changed to director of business and finance. Fink believed that Bedore's strengths helped to offset his own. "I was a poor politician," Fink confessed (Terence Smith). He credited Bedore with the raising of $50,000 in working capital for the college in 1965. According to Fink, Bedore's hiring "turned out to be one of the wisest decisions we've ever made" (Terence Smith). Against many challenges, Fink helped to change the dream into reality.

Need for a Campus

After Fink was hired, a major decision was where to place the campus. There was a strong proposal from the community of Greenville that it be placed there. However, there was equally strong feeling that the campus should be at a geographic location that could better serve the needs of the entire service area, in keeping with the MAISD proposal. The board considered both the factors of location in addition to road access (county-wide accessibility). Because this decision was so controversial, the board decided to hire consultants to make the final recommendation. The consultants were a professor from Michigan State University, Dr. Max Smith, and a professor from the University of Michigan, Dr. Raymond Young. There were 18 sites proposed by various sources. One was near Dickerson Lake, another was Stanton as the county seat, yet another was the corner of M66 and M57. The consultants made the recommendation of the Anderson Farm on Sidney Road just east of Sidney, but that proposal was not one of the 18! Key factors were this site's central location, and some proximity to Ionia County, since that county had voted down a proposal for its own community college.

Given the recommendation of Smith and Young, the board selected the Sidney site of the Anderson Farm as the location of the new college campus in September 1965. Daverman Associates was the firm selected as the architect for the initial college campus buildings. The board adopted the initial master plan for the college, developed by Daverman Associates. This plan called for initial construction of four buildings: a learning resource center, vocational-technical building, science and arts center (Instruction East), and student center. It also included a grassy courtyard, called the Atrium of Learning, which could be used for student gatherings, outdoor commencements, and sports events. Because the Roman term "atrium" was used, the mascot for later MCC sports teams became the Centurion. This initial phase of construction was designed to accommodate 550 students.

The campus student center, however, was subsequently dropped from the initial list at this time. *The Daily News* explained in January 1966:

> The Montcalm Community College Board of Trustees Monday night voted to drop one building from the first phase of construction in order to assure funds for the vocational-technical building.
>
> Construction of the campus center, which will be the hub of student activity, will be delayed. Some areas originally scheduled for this building will be incorporated in the lower level of the learning center.
>
> At such time as the campus center can be constructed the lower level of the learning center can be changed in accord with the original design. (Leach)

In addition to this bit of a disappointment, MCC learned a month later that the funds it counted on from the Higher Education Facilities Act (HEFA) were not being granted. A total of $774,000 had been expected to help finance the campus building projects. "This is certainly bad news," President Fink stated, "but this is not going to crush us. The college will open in September, 1967, as scheduled" (Leach). The

HEFA funds were part of $1,860,616 needed to finance the first phase of campus building.

Business Manager Bedore began work immediately with the law firm of Miller, Canfield, Paddock and Stone of Grand Rapids to arrange for the sale of bonds in the amount of approximately $1 million. Board Treasurer Doser explained this was necessary also because the first tax levy would need to be used mostly for operational purposes over a period of 21 months. Thankfully, the college did learn at the time that it would be eligible for federal soil bank funds for not growing corn on 10 acres of its campus.

Early Planning and Costs

In the meantime, the board announced that a few college classes would be offered at various locations throughout the county starting in the fall of 1966 during construction of the campus, and authorized President Fink to employ a vocational dean. That first dean was Maurice Swift, hired in February 1966. Several part-time instructors were also hired, including Morford for political science, and Frank Fishell for mathematics. At first, the college used offices at the MAISD building in Stanton, but as soon as the campus was purchased, the Anderson farmhouse was converted into office space for the earliest administrators and faculty, and for board meetings.

By April 1966, the college determined to temporarily house the majority of its classes in the Central Montcalm Public School District, and had established tuition and fees for its opening semester. Those would be:

Resident tuition - $8.50 per credit hour
Non-resident tuition - $13.50 per credit hour
Resident VoTech - $127.50 per semester
Non-resident VoTech - $202.50 per semester

A resident student who took a normal 15-credit load would pay $255 per year in tuition, and a non-resident would pay $505 per year.

"Back in 1966, the college initially offered two [complete] programs – nursing and auto mechanics," reported *The Daily News*. "Unfortunately for the auto mechanics students, there wasn't a conventional place for them to meet. So classes were conducted in a cell at the Montcalm County Jail in Stanton" (Cole, Dec. 27, 2005). According to Doser, "The jail was new and they didn't have all the cells filled." Doser joked that students were encouraged not to misbehave. She said, "They were warned that they would have to be at the jail 24 hours a day, not just for class" (Cole).

Curriculum, Infrastructure, and First Enrolled

Fink asked Morford to help establish the original general studies curriculum. "We called a one-day Saturday conference in pedagogy at Greenville High School to generate ideas," Morford remembers. At Fink's suggestion, early courses were given similar catchy, though male-oriented names that would not bode well in the 21st century. For example, social science was called "Man's Social World," and physical science was called "Man's Physical World." These titles were used until 1976. When developed, the first curriculum included:

Basic Communication – 2 semesters
Introduction to Literature – 2 semesters
College Writing – 2 semesters
Mathematics for General Education – 1 semester
College Algebra – 1 semester
Elementary Analysis – 1 semester
Calculus – 1 semester
Political Science – 2 semesters
General Psychology – 1 semester
Child Psychology – 1 semester
Modern European History – 2 semesters
Geography – 1 semester
Physical Geography – 1 semester

A proposed operating budget for 1966-67 was approved, calling for total expenditures of $54,027.50 from a total available fund of $54,660. This was significantly more than the 1965-66 budget of $36,634. The board also authorized the printing of 3,000 brochures to distribute to high school students and other prospective students. The brochure included a description of the college and its curriculum. All incoming students would be required to take the American College Test (ACT).

Preparations for the start of the school in fall of 1966 escalated rapidly. Bedore was transferred from administrative assistant to business manager, Jo Ann Regis was employed as director of nursing, and the first full-time instructors were hired: John Dargitz as instructor in Drafting and Design Technology, Gary Moore as instructor of Auto Mechanics, and Helen Brehm as instructor of Executive Secretarial Science. Mary Helms was also employed as the secretary to the vocational dean.

As plans for campus development continued, the board requested that Sidney Township build or cause to be built the road from Sidney Road into the campus. At first, the drive was to be named Anderson Memorial Drive in honor of Alma Anderson and her late husband, E. V. Anderson, who owned the farm prior to its conversion to the college campus. Later, the name College Drive was favored. "The name, 'Anderson Lane,' however, would continue to be used for the path leading from the Barn to the campus in honor of the Anderson Family" (Lantz, 2013).

By May 1966, applicants for student enrollment for the fall were accepted in the following programs:

Practical Nursing
Automotive Mechanics
Agriculture
Power Technology
Drafting and Design Technology
Office Occupations
Academics (General Studies)

The first applicant to the college was Vicki Bartholomew of Lakeview, for the Licensed Practical Nursing program. As the program added applicants, Ruth Rose and Ipha Fishell were added to the full-time nursing faculty.

More infrastructure was put into place. John Carlson was employed as director of the learning resource center, and the board allocated $5,000 to begin acquisition of library materials to be housed on the main level of the new Administration Building, with staff offices in the basement. The board also voted to take over the responsibility for apprentice training, previously sponsored by Greenville Public Schools.

First Classes and Campus Development

The first MCC classes began August 29, 1966. Due to limited enrollment, the agriculture and power technology classes were cancelled. But other enrollments were encouraging. There were 90 enrolled in the apprenticeship classes, 25 in Practical Nursing, 22 in Office Occupations, 15 in Drafting and Design, and 25 in Academics (General Studies) for a total student body of 177.

Campus development continued as well, with the additional purchase of 80 acres, raising the college site to 238 acres. Bids for construction of the first MCC buildings were awarded to Gust Construction of Cedar Springs, and a groundbreaking ceremony was held September 26, with Governor George Romney participating. Daverman Associates was responsible for arranging the governor's appearance as part of his two-day tour of west Michigan. More than 1,000 people gathered to witness the official start of construction. The governor called the speedy progress of the school a fine example of what citizen involvement can do.

By spring, enrollments jumped to 229 and continued to grow. In February 1967, preliminary plans were also approved for the building of the Vocational-Technical Building (now called Instruction North). The building would resemble an industrial shop with high ceilings and open floor space. Designed initially to provide teaching area for the automotive mechanics program by fall 1967, the facility would also be equipped with floor exhaust and drain systems.

During the first academic year, a number of significant positions were staffed in anticipation of the 1967 opening of MCC's campus. These included full-time faculty members: Fishell (mathematics), John Pastoor (language arts), Vernon Blake (language arts), Barbara Goretzka (language arts), Kenneth Smith (science), Morford (social science),

Gerald Freid (social science), and Arthur Keinberger (automotive). Robert Tupper was employed as the first dean of students, Frank Reeder as maintenance superintendent, Phyllis Durbin as administrative secretary to the dean of students, Verla Cummings as half-time assistant librarian, and Carlson as librarian. The board was also increased from six to seven, and Orville Trebian was appointed as the newest trustee.

Ken Smith recalls, "I had quite a surprise when I came to interview for the science instructor position at MCC. When I went to the president's office in the farmhouse, I had no idea the president was Dr. Don Fink, who had been my music teacher at Alma High School." Smith continues, "All I could think of was how strongly he had scolded me one night after a concert, when some BBs, a rubber band, and a bobby pin fell out of my shirt pocket that let him know I was a naughty student who shot BBs at fellow students! Thankfully, I still got the job" (K. Smith).

First Commencement Services

Two commencement services were conducted in the summer of 1967. MCC's first graduation exercise was held June 9, 1967, at 8 p.m. in the lecture-study of Greenville High School. All of the 30 graduates were members of the Tool and Die Apprenticeship Program. Dr. Robert C. Lusk, Director of Educational Services for the Automobile Manufacturers Association of Detroit served as the featured commencement speaker, along with three other speakers: Sydney Swainston, Instructor Morford, and Dean of Vocational-Technical Studies Swift. The first graduates were: Theodore Albert, Ted Cowles, Thomas Fagerlin, Paul Lucas, Dennis McPhee, Duane Miller, Jerry Miller, John Peck, Peter Schantz, Richard VanHoose, Reuel Rockafellow, Kenneth Bissell, Ray Harris, Richard Johnson, Ronald Johnson, Bruce Lund, Michael Rittersdorf, Richard Warner, Darwin Jensen, Roger Bush, Terry Clements, Harold Swindell, Gerald Yost, Kenneth Keeler, Terry McPhee, Alden Neitzel, Keith Phelps, and Dale James. Graduates from Greenville Tool and Die were presented their certificates by Ash, the company's president, and chair of the MCC Board of Trustees.

The second commencement service of the first academic year took place July 21, 1967, at 8 p.m. in the sanctuary of the Congregational

13

Church of Greenville for those graduating from the practical nursing program. A total of 23 graduates received their diplomas from Dean of Vocational-Technical Studies Maurice Swift, and were pinned by Director of Practical Nursing Regis. MCC was affiliated with three area hospitals at the time, from which students gained their clinical experience: Carson City Hospital, United Memorial Hospital in Greenville, and Kelsey Memorial Hospital in Lakeview. Each graduate became eligible to take the Michigan Board of Nurse Examiner's exam to become licensed to practice.

Forming of the Library

Verla Cummings was hired to assist Carlson in the creation of MCC's library. Her first six months, beginning in July 1967, were spent in a rented lodge building in Sidney, ordering books from faculty-provided lists, and "putting them in boxes somewhat according to their Dewey decimal classifications." She graphically remembers, "The building was bee-infested in the summer, and very cold as winter came. John, Eleanor Piper and I sat with our coats on, and our feet on boxes to keep them off the cold floor, and shivered" (Cummings, 2004).

New Campus Opens

Classes began for the first time on MCC's new campus with the fall semester of 1967, although students met with their instructors in Central Montcalm High School for the initial week while the buildings were being finished. The first semester saw enrollments of 153 full-time students, 63 part-time students, and 100 in the apprenticeship program, for a total of 316. Of the full-time students, 54 were in general academic studies and the remainder were in the various vocational programs, with practical nursing, auto mechanics, and office work leading the way.

Again, Cummings muses, "Finally, the campus was almost ready to open, and we had our brand new library space in the Administration Building. However, for some reason, the shelves had not yet been delivered, so the books were propped in rows on the floor. For weeks, we had to creep or crawl through the rows of arranged books to find the correct number until the shelves finally arrived" (Cummings, 2004).

A campus dedication ceremony was joyfully held September 26, 1967, with Lt. Gov. William Milliken as the featured speaker.

As already noted, the first building constructed was the administration building, but the administration was downstairs and the library was housed upstairs. Years later, the library was moved downstairs and the administration upstairs, due to the weight of the books and need for greater accessibility to the administrative offices.

Next was the two-story classroom building, now called Instruction East. Most all of the general studies classes were held in the two-story classroom building. The vocational building, or auto mechanics building (now called Instruction North), was among the first three to be completed and dedicated. Some of the early commencements were also held in Instruction North. Morford recalls that his parents actually sat on the car lift in the building during one of the early commencements. Outdoor commencements were conducted in the central campus area east of the Administration Building, known as the aforementioned atrium.

During the first academic year on the school's new campus, several other key decisions were made:

- Crosby was named chairperson of the board.
- Morford was elected chairman of the academic faculty and appointed acting Dean of academic studies.
- Herbert Hood was employed as an instructor in business education.
- Heinz Radtke was hired as a full-time welding instructor.
- The board authorized the creation of an MCC interscholastic basketball team, and appointed Larry Peterson as coach. Home games would be played at Central Montcalm High School.
- The MCC College Choir made its first public appearance under the direction of Science Instructor Smith.
- Final plans were approved for the construction of a one-story classroom building, today called Instruction West. Again, K. Smith recalls:

> I personally believe that several extracurricular and co-curricular activities greatly enhanced the regular

curriculum and helped many students develop their talents, establish lasting friendships, and provided the opportunity for them to belong to a meaningful group ... Thus, the formation of the college choir, and later jazz (stage) band, men and women's ensembles, and barbershop groups in the early years of the college's existence served to reinforce the positive attributes." (K. Smith, 2013, written)

First On-Campus Commencement

The first on-campus commencement took place at the Sidney campus on Wednesday, May 22, 1968, at 7:15 p.m. Although several apprentices and practical nurses graduated from the college in 1967, this marked the first time associate degrees were awarded and the first commencement for graduates of the academic division.

All staff and members of the Board of Trustees were in full academic garb, and graduates wore the traditional caps and gowns. The speaker for the occasion was Dr. Daryl Pendergraft, assistant to the president and executive dean at the University of Northern Iowa.

Fink presided over the commencement ceremony, which was conducted in MCC's outdoor atrium. A brief reception followed in the student commons. The first graduates who received degrees were: Helen Hamler, Steve Foster, and Tarry Stearns. (See photo at the end of Chapter 8.)

Growing Support Staff

Lois Springsteen began her employment at MCC in May 1968, when she was hired as secretary to the business manager, Bedore.

"Don Fink and Cliff Bedore were totally different, but I admired them both," Springsteen reports. "Don was very professional, and had high goals. Cliff was a businessman and highly involved in the financial well-being of the college. Together, they were a good team, and I was so pleased to be a part of it in my support role" (Springsteen, 2014).

In her new capacity, Springsteen served as a receptionist/switchboard operator, accounts receivable clerk, and representative of the business office during registration. Springsteen later became the college's first administrative assistant. She assisted the president, coordinated personnel relations, provided public information, and served as secretary to the board. While employed fulltime, she earned her associate degree from MCC and bachelor's degree from Central Michigan University, and taught in the college's prison program at Ionia, known as COPE (College Opportunity Prison Education). She continued in ever-expanding roles until her retirement in 1986. She reflects, "I received so much gratification from every aspect of my time at MCC, and enjoyed working with so many wonderful people" (Springsteen, 2014).

Community Engagement and Student Activities

The new college not only sensed the needs of students, but also sought creative ways to bring learning and development to the greater community. One such measure was the inauguration in 1968 of The Critical Issues Series, a lectureship open to the public, intended to stimulate thought and personal enrichment. During the next several years, the series featured a variety of guest speakers and topics. Some of those included Dr. Edward Jacomo of the Alma College art department, speaking on the effects of mass media; and Dr. Fred Alexander, headmaster of the Leelanau Schools of Glen Arbor, addressing the question, "Can Man Save Himself? The Role of Education."

During the 1969-70 academic year, students could attend the lectures for credit, and members of the community could purchase a season pass ticket. Other speakers included Frederick Currier, president of Market Opinion Research in Detroit, on the topic, "Are the Polls Telling You How to Think?"; Dr. Gerald McIntosh addressing "Black Power and Integration"; and Dr. Gilbert Davis of Grand Valley State University speaking on "Equities and Inequities of [Draft] Deferment." As part of the community learning initiative, Howard Bernson was employed as MCC's first community services director.

A student senate also began in 1968 with Mark Hansen of Ionia as president, Mark Cole of Ionia as vice president, Sheila Herald of Stanton as secretary and Sandy Peterman of Sheridan as treasurer. It is interesting to note that Cole was a resident of the Michigan Reformatory attending MCC on a release program. Student-centered education was one of the concerns expressed by Fink when he gave his state of the college addresses. One such address in 1969 stressed the need for a "freewheeling approach" to providing education.

Student activities began to flourish on the young campus. In February 1969, Sharon VanHoose of Greenville was named Centurion Sweetheart at a basketball evening. In the first game, the Kalamazoo Valley Community College faculty defeated the MCC faculty 28-17, and the Kalamazoo varsity defeated the MCC varsity 102-81. During the same semester, Academic Dean Morford proposed a study skills center for students, which was established the following summer in the large conference room of the Learning Resource Center (Library), with Pastoor assigned as the director.

Early Expansion – Instruction West

In August 1969, final touches were added to the new one-story classroom building, which opened in time for the new semester. Seating arrangements for 401 students and office space for an additional six faculty members was provided in the new facility, the second academic classroom building to be erected since the college began operation.

"We are now in the process of purchasing equipment and furnishings for the new building and hope to have it almost completed by the August 18 date," reported Bedore. "We plan to spend about $25,000 for the furnishings, which will provide the latest equipment available to our students" (MCC news release, August 7, 1969). Two of the lecture rooms were designed as auditoriums, and built on step levels for better student viewing and hearing, with seating arranged in a half-circle. The larger auditorium seated 135, while the smaller accommodated 96 students and desk-tables.

Interestingly, a story was later told about how Keeping Posted was selected as the name for the MCC employee newsletter.

"When the Sidney campus was first built, there was a concern that people might drive their vehicles on the sidewalk that runs between the Administration/Library Building and Instruction West. Accordingly, a concrete-filled post was placed in the center of the sidewalk between the two buildings. Students and staff would often tape notices, flyers, etc. to the post, using it as sort of a kiosk. The post was later removed. However, when a name was needed for the employee newsletter, 'Keeping Posted' was chosen in commemoration of that post" (Lantz, email, October 31, 2013).

Springsteen was the creator of Keeping Posted, and still has a copy of the very first edition. "I'm somewhat amazed to learn it is still going on today, and I feel proud to have launched it" (Springsteen, 2014).

MCC also applied to the state to inquire about the possibility of dorms or faculty housing in 1969, considering the isolation of the Anderson Farm. Early press releases from the school often referred to MCC as "Sidney-based." As a case in point, when a *Grand Rapids Press* reporter asked to meet with Morford about the question of housing he asked, "Where is Sidney?"

Morford replied, "Sir, you just came through it on the way here! We're an oasis in the middle of the Montcalm cornfield" (Morford, 2012).

Morford continued to explain to the reporter that there was an early assumption that faculty members wanted to live on campus. But when MCC applied to the state for housing consideration, the state didn't agree, and people didn't mind driving. Students, faculty and staff were willing to drive from locations throughout the county, and the board soon passed a policy to provide mileage for adjunct instructors. Dorms were never constructed. The apartments across Sidney Road were not built by MCC, but because of MCC. A private enterprise learned that the school's request was denied by the state and seized an opportunity. When the apartments were first constructed, students did make use of them. Over the years, however, the college students occupied fewer of the apartment units.

Fostering School Spirit

During the 1969 fall semester, MCC fielded an intercollegiate cross-country team, and announced the following appointments: Blake as dramatics coach, Smith as official choir director, Don Mullins as student government advisor, and Frank Fedewa as basketball coach. Smith was also named director of the MCC Pep Band for $200, and Larry Taylor was named cross-country coach for $350. The board also approved the creation of a student newspaper to be called, The Post.

Smith and Don Stearns took interested students on a weekend trip to northern Michigan in the spring of 1969 to participate in a variety of outdoor activities, including hiking nature trails and outdoor gymnastic events. This became an annual spring event for years to come.

In a move to foster student spirit, permission was granted by the board to permit students to locate a Snoopy likeness on the southeast corner of campus. The MCC Centurions basketball team embarked on a 25-game season, playing "home" games in Edmore, Greenville, Alma, Lakeview, Central Montcalm, Carson City, Ionia, Vestaburg, and St. Louis. In addition, MCC's Drama Club presented its first three-act play, *The Apple Tree* in Auditorium 1 of the newly constructed one-story classroom building (Instruction West).

Student activities continued to flourish in 1970, with the basketball team finishing its season with a 17-10 record, establishment of the MCC baseball team under Coach Petersen with nine games scheduled, and the official launch of the MCC golf team coached by Mullins. Dean of Students Tupper chaperoned a group of MCC students on a canoe outing, and saved the life of a boy who nearly drowned. Tupper received a special commendation by the MCC board. The college choir also began performing in regular concerts, such as the Swing into Spring concert.

By August 1970, the board gave its official approval to the remodeling of the barn into a Barn Theater and allocated $2,000 for renovations, based on a plan submitted by Blake, college dramatics coach.

"Not only will the College benefit from this, but also the whole community," explained Fink. "We are hoping for the support of the whole community and also wide community usage" (MCC news release August 13, 1970). However, student use of the building continued to be the key focus of the quaintly remodeled structure.

Six nationally known individuals and touring groups were highlighted in the lecture/concert series offered during the 1970-71 academic year. The board also adopted a student activity eligibility requirement policy, employed Darwin Sampson as the advisor to *The*

Post student newspaper, and authorized the launch of MCC's squad with eight female students selected as the cheerleaders for the Centurion basketball team.

During the fall 1970 semester, a campus organization called MCC Student Volunteers was formed on campus, and the student government held an ox roast for the public with 900 in attendance, each paying $1. The pep band became the official MCC Stage Band, with Smith conducting at a stipend of $300. The board approved the purchase of several instruments, and in February 1971, Smith organized the MCC Community Band, which held its first concert at Central Montcalm High School. At the same time, Fink organized a community chorus that presented an April concert at the Stanton Congregational Church. The chorus was conducted by President Fink with the assistance of Smith. Sixty voices performed *The Crucifixion*. In addition, the MCC Players performed three one-act plays. One was titled, *Will the Real Jesus Christ Please Stand Up?*

Ups and Downs

These years did not only see the development of student activities. MCC began to offer classes in the state prisons located in Ionia. It also applied for and won a state grant of $100,000 to expand the Vocational-Technical Building, and added an aviation power plant mechanics program to the college curriculum. Morford well remembers planes landing on the field next to what is today called Heritage Village. The college faculty voted to affiliate with the Michigan Education Association, and MCC announced the creation of a speaker's bureau, under which MCC would make speakers available to community organizations. These would largely be faculty members and administrators. Summer school was launched, and more than 100 graduates continued to walk in commencement up to the fourth annual ceremony in spring of 1971.

However, the young school was faced with some tough financial struggles and resulting tough decisions. In February 1971, MCC lost its millage election to increase the operating millage from 1 to 1.5 mills. The board's March meeting lasted from 7:30 p.m. to 1:37 a.m. as the trustees attempted to deal with the financial crunch. As a result,

MCC dropped its shared time program with area high schools, and the board voted to not offer a contract for the librarian position held by Cummings. The board also voted not to renew the contract of Counselor Robert Gravelle or retain the services of Jo Vanderhoff as the school's part-time public relations reporter. However, it did rescind the action, and offered contracts again to Cummings and Gravelle. Every possible cost-cutting strategy was sought to save resources. Fink even asked all faculty members to run dittographic tests on the back of the previous week's tests.

Faced with these challenges and his own new opportunities, President Fink submitted his resignation in May of 1971. John Stafford nicely summarizes his legacy in *The Daily News* article titled Timely leadership at MCC.

> Fink was the founding president of MCC, assuming the leadership role in June of 1965 and continuing until 1971. He was an outgoing, energetic, creative chief executive who spared no effort to promote the interests of the institution. Although the college received a lukewarm greeting from some areas within its district, Fink never stopped trying to win these hearts over. And he became a pro at knowing where to go in Lansing or Washington for added funding.
>
> In the middle years, Fink was on the road a substantial amount of the time, knocking on bureaucratic doors pleading the case of MCC and its financial needs. Without Fink's willingness and talent in this area, one can only speculate whether the college would have achieved its present physical size. (Stafford)

Despite Fink's resignation, college life continued. MCC received a grant from the state of Michigan to establish an Area Educational Vocational Guidance Center. Gravelle was appointed as director of the new center, and the board named Bedore as MCC's interim president, and Burns as counselor.

MONTCALM
COUNTY
COMMUNITY
COLLEGE
STUDY

FINAL REPORT
OF THE
CITIZENS STUDY COUNCIL

STUDY COORDINATED BY
THE OFFICE OF
COMMUNITY COLLEGE COOPERATION
MICHIGAN STATE UNIVERSITY

JUNE 1964

Front cover of the 64-page feasibility study prepared by
the Montcalm County Citizens Advisory Council

Top: MCC's first Board of Trustees included, from left, James Crosby, Joseph Cook, Harold Steele, Stanley Ash (Chair), Grace Greenhoe, and Beatrice Doser. Bottom: Dr. Donald Fink, MCC's first president

Leslie Morford, first instructor employed by MCC

Groundbreaking for the college campus with
Gov. George Romney in 1966

Top: MCC's Sidney campus as it appeared in 1967;
Bottom: Barn converted to the Barn Theater in 1970

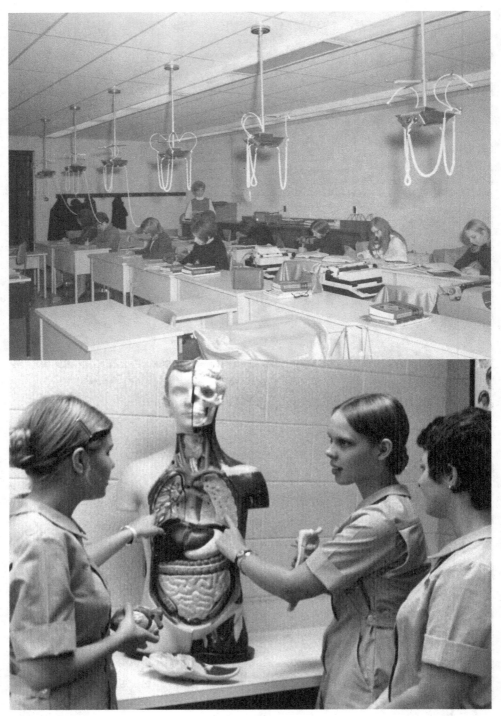

Top: Early transcription class;
Bottom: Early nursing students learn anatomy and physiology.

Top: Early nursing commencement held at the Congregational Church of Greenville, July 21, 1967, with program director Jo Ann Regis pinning the graduates; Bottom: Trustee Francis Rivard awards diplomas as Dean Dennis Mulder reads names at a vocational commencement in the Vocational-Technical Building.

Top: Basketball Coach Frank Fedewa with an early basketball team (late 1960s/early 1970s); Bottom: Coach Larry Taylor with an early cross-country team (late 1960s/early 1970s).

Top: MCC's Marathon Men as featured in the *Guinness Book of World Records*; Bottom: Counselor Donald Mullins served as MCC's golf coach.

Chapter 2

Building a Team

According to Chairperson James Crosby, the Board of Trustees elected to make an interim presidential appointment for the 1971-72 year to provide time to seek a long-term solution for the college's financial situation. "Dr. Bedore has first-hand knowledge of the problem and possible courses of action," said Crosby (MCC news release, June 23, 1971). After serving briefly as a finance consultant in the state Department of Education while completing his doctoral coursework at Michigan State University, Cliff Bedore was first appointed MCC's administrative assistant in August 1965, as noted earlier. In 1967, his title was changed to business manager. Four years later, he became the college's interim president.

Bedore received his EdD from Michigan State University in June 1968. Prior to his studies at MSU, Bedore taught science and served as an athletic coach for 16 years in West Branch, and was then appointed superintendent of schools in Sault Ste. Marie Township for three years. His new responsibilities as interim president at MCC began August 1, 1971.

Beatrice Doser was elected as the chairperson of the Board of Trustees in July of 1971, a position she held for many years to come. And during the same month, a young man named Don Burns was employed as a counselor in the Area Vocational Guidance Center. He remembers coming to a campus that had just experienced a significant turnover and downsizing.

Bill Braman has fond memories of Doser and "her amazing leadership ability" (Braman, 2014). "Bea was a remarkable woman," he recounts. "She had a very quiet way about her, but she was a true visionary and knew how to get the job done."

Bedore navigated through a variety of advances and setbacks during the early months of his interim presidency, seeking to bring stability to the new institution. His steady, quiet, and business-like approach was different than the more outgoing and aggressive leadership style of his predecessor. This was what the college needed at that time.

Renovations for the Barn Theater required more funds than originally thought, and the board allocated an additional $3,000 for the makeover. However, the board also voted to delay by one year the application for accreditation by the North Central Accrediting Association, due to the financial difficulties MCC was encountering. North Central concurred with the decision to delay, and granted MCC the ongoing status of "recognized candidate" (MCC board minutes).

Trustees decided to set a new millage rate at 1 mill for operation and .5 mills for debt retirement, but after further deliberation a month later, decided not to seek an additional millage at the time.

As during any presidential change, there followed other changes in leadership as well. James Kirk became the new dean of student services, and Robert Gravelle was named as dean of academic studies. Additional counselors and admissions aides were added as fall enrollments for 1971 showed 342 full-time and 222 part-time students.

The 1971-72 lecture and concert series opened with a lecture on drugs by renowned performer and author Art Linkletter. Finances for Linkletter and 13 other programs slated during the season were assisted by funds from the Kellogg Foundation. One of the concerts featured the University of Michigan Symphonic Band performing in Greenville.

At the same time, the board authorized acquisition of surplus aircraft for use in the aviation mechanics program, and an additional $4,600 for the Barn Theater. And work began on the development of nature trails on college property and the state land behind the college.

In March 1972, MCC sponsored a countywide creative writing contest, open to all high school students in the college district. Prizes were offered in poetry, drama and short story. The first prize in each category was a $125 scholarship to MCC. This contest is still held annually. The board also established an Outstanding Alumnus Award and Distinguished Service Award, to recognize an area citizen who has made an outstanding contribution to MCC.

Still faced with financial concerns, the board set a June 12, 1972, election to seek an increase in operational millage from one mill to two mills. It also discussed the financial challenges of running the basketball program. Funds for the program had been coming from the student activity fund, but that was becoming less feasible. The board considered taking funds from the general fund, depending on the outcome of the millage election.

Second President Appointed

MCC's fifth commencement saw 105 students receive degrees or certificates, and the board received letters from the Faculty Council, secretarial staff and administrators commending Bedore for his handling of the double duties of president and business manager. As a result, the trustees asked Bedore to accept the official presidency of the college in June 1972, and Frank Fishell was named business manager. Bedore accepted and served as MCC's president until 1978.

According to Burns, "President Bedore had many challenges to wade through, and he handled them well" (Burns, 2012). Of course, the biggest challenge was the school's fiscal position. There simply was not enough revenue to do what needed to be done. "President Bedore brought fiscal balance and stability. Contract bargaining also began under Bedore's leadership, and he played a steady hand" (Burns, 2012).

Bedore also made it a point to engage more of the community. Under his leadership the Activities Building was constructed and the pool was installed. More and more children and senior citizens frequented the campus and viewed MCC as "their" college.

MCC's Adolescence

Burns views the college as in its infancy during the years of President Donald Fink, and in its adolescence during the era of President Bedore.

"It was during these years the school began to mature and establish its identity. It also had the challenges of adolescence to face in the process. It was also like building a team" (Burns meeting).

"Colleges are places that focus on students," Burns explains. "In the earliest years, MCC began with a pretty traditional way of thinking – 18- to 23-year-olds taking basic transfer courses and courses for work. But over the years, the student body changed. By the late 1960s we uniquely got involved with training prison inmates. We at one time probably had more inmate students than students on campus" (Burns). Most of the work was in the Ionia prisons, teaching traditional courses.

Burns continues to explain that in the early 1970s, MCC also had quite a few Vietnam vets. Another group of students was identified as CETA (Comprehensive Employment and Training Act) employees. The nearby Lyons Chrysler Plant closed, and 800 displaced workers needed retraining. Many of those came to MCC for workforce training and development.

Curriculum saw modifications as well. It began as a basic format in general studies along with some vocational and technical programming. Over time, the college developed curricula that looked carefully at community needs, rather than what the leaders thought they were or had an interest in. The school learned to get better connected with K-12 curriculum and other institutions of higher learning so that transfer worked better for students and graduates. Even the schedule became more user-focused with time. In the earliest days, classes were scheduled at a specific time and place during the weekdays, not in the evenings or weekends, and the Sidney campus was the location for most classes. Through the years, more courses were offered outside these perimeters, and the curriculum changed.

Aviation Power Mechanics and Developing Programs

A unique program begun early in the 1970s was aviation power mechanics, but it lasted for less than a decade. Jesse Fox was the aviation instructor and later became the vocational dean. MCC owned a plane that often took off from and landed on the field that is now adjacent to Heritage Village. Les Morford remembers giving a speech at an event in that field when Bedore was president, and jokingly said as the plane was taking off, "Don't mess with Dr. Bedore or he will bomb you!" (Morford, 2012).

Fox reflects, "I came to MCC after my time at the University of Illinois and St. Louis University before that. I actually took a class in community colleges from a man named Dr. Monroe, a founding father of the idea, and it ignited a flame in me. Now, I was absolutely delighted to lead the new school's aviation program, and later serve as dean" (Fox, 2014).

MCC had been established as a college in the 1960s farming community, with an emphasis on agriculture. But even that changed with time. The community and college moved more into manufacturing and health care. This brought several modifications. For example, some of the early commencements and special programs were held at 8 p.m. to allow farm workers to finish their chores. As the complexion of the people shifted, the times for most of these changed to 7 p.m. The service sectors, prisons, and health care providers became the largest employers. As the community changed, so did MCC's marching orders. With the energy crisis of the early 1970s, the schedule was adjusted so that classes were basically conducted Monday through Thursday, though the offices remained open five days a week.

"Community colleges in the 1960s were basically considered junior colleges," Burns states. "During the 1960s, the shift came to community colleges." With the changing focus and student demographic, the nature of MCC's board, faculty, and staff, naturally changed as well. Burns explains,

> When I arrived in 1971, board members were in their 30s and 40s. Staff members were in their 20s and 30s. It was a very young staff. And the college was going through its institutional adolescence. Today, 50 years later, the college has matured. We have an older board, with some in their 60s and 70s. Hopefully, youthful innovation remains, but the institution is more mature. (Burns, 2013)

Student-Led Initiatives

Being a young campus at the time, it was quite open to youthful initiatives. An example of this was when student council members decided to sponsor a rock concert on campus in 1974 and sought approval from the board to invite the band Grass Roots. At first, the board said no. Trustees were fearful of what behavior might erupt at the campus event, which would lead to bad public relations. They also expressed other concerns, like the fear of another Woodstock. The students were upset. In an effort to appeal their case, the students circulated petitions among the community and tried to deal with all of the objections the Board of Trustees raised (toilet facilities, security, and behavior). To the credit of both groups, the trustees changed their vote of 4-3 against the concert to 5-2 in favor. The concert ran smoothly and problem-free, but it was not well attended. Students lost $4,500 despite charging a modest admission fee.

Another unique idea during the Bedore era emerged from the basketball team. The team sought to be in the *Guinness Book of World Records* for having played the longest basketball game in world history. Team members contacted Guinness to determine how long it would need to be and what rules needed to be enforced (such as how many substitutes could be used, how frequently breaks could be taken, etc.). The appointed day finally arrived, and the MCC Centurions played a continuous basketball game for 62 hours. The accomplishment was recorded in the *Guiness Book of World Records*. Only one person stayed in the stands the whole time cheering on the players, and that was Burns, who was dean of students at the time.

Tragedy Strikes

Sadly, there were also some tragic events in the 1970s, including the murder of an MCC student by another student. A student of Morford's, Robert Lee Crum, was thought to be challenged with psychological imbalance (Morford, 2012). He reportedly began to fantasize that his father, who owned a clothing store, was a colonel in the U.S. Air Force and would fly his plane over the MCC campus. He was said to have also fantasized that he was a drug agent, and began to spread that word around campus and the apartments across the street where he lived. Unfortunately, there were other students living in the apartments who were allegedly drug users. One of those was Timothy Christenson (Daily News, 1973). When he learned there was a "drug agent" just down the hall, it caused serious concern. As a result, he used a coat hanger to strangle him. Crum's body was later discovered in Wabasis Creek, south of Greenville (Daily News, 1973). Morford attended much of the trial in Stanton. He recalls very distinctly that the prosecution showed a notebook that had the large letters written on it, EOANA, which was believed to stand for "End of Another Narcotics Agent" (Morford). The prosecutor entered this as evidence. Christenson was incarcerated and put into the state prison at Ionia. Morford later had Christenson as a student in the prison when the college had a prison program.

College Resilience

Despite the understandable shock and grief felt by the MCC family, life at the institution pressed on. Instructor Morford was selected to direct a study of senior citizens in Montcalm County. The result of this study led to the founding and funding of the Montcalm County Commission on Aging. In addition, the Area Vocational Guidance Center received federal funding for an additional year, enabling Burns to continue as a counselor in the center. Classes continued at the Michigan Training Unit and Michigan Reformatory in Ionia, with the rate of pay for instructors set at $275.

With an ongoing focus on student concerns, the board authorized the use of $1,300 to initiate a tutoring program. It also agreed to have the college offer the course Contemporary Sex Problems. In addition, the board provided one tuition scholarship for a basketball player from each in-district high school and voted to approve the existence of a residential construction program for the 1973-74 academic year. However, since there were no applicants for the tool and design program, that program was eliminated.

The school also continued to recognize alumni and community members active in the pursuits of MCC.

Alma Mater

In October 1973, MCC's Alma Mater was written by Science Instructor Kenneth Smith (music) and English Instructor Vernon Blake (lyrics) in the Instruction West Building. It was later revised by Smith.

> Amid the fields of Michigan there shines a brighter hue
> Where sons and daughters of Montcalm bring their dreams so true.
> Fields of green and golden sun hold our hearts in years to come.
> In years to come, keep fresh and green the dream of our Montcalm.

Later, the University of Michigan Men's Glee Club was asked to perform and record the MCC Alma Mater, which is now played at each induction ceremony of MCC's Alpha Tau Alpha chapter of the Phi Theta Kappa Honor Society. It has also been performed by the MCC choir at every commencement since it was written.

K. Smith muses:

> As "Duke" [Vernon] Blake stated so cogently in our MCC Alma Mater lyrics many years ago, "where sons and daughters of Montcalm bring their dreams so true," this institution has been here to fulfill the dreams of many people over the years and will be here "for years to come." It is up to all college personnel to "keep fresh and green the dream of our Montcalm." (K. Smith, typed reflection, 2013)

The Dream Continues

Dennis Mulder was given a year's leave of absence from his teaching position in 1973 to direct the College Opportunity Prison Education (COPE) program, which he founded and named, and Burns was appointed director of the Area Guidance Center, replacing Gravelle who asked to be relieved of that position. MCC administration, in partnership with the board, also cultivated the plans for the multi-purpose building, which would eventually be called the Activities Building.

In 1974, MCC adopted an affirmative action policy, and was granted full accreditation from the North Central Association. The board approved a women's basketball team and women's volleyball interscholastic program, and Burns became the dean of students and community services.

Innovations were also tested in the delivery of education. The social science course SS100 was offered during the summer session via local radio. Students received lectures via radio and met once each week on campus for discussion and testing. Morford served as the instructor, bringing both radio and television instruction to MCC that he pioneered at Central Michigan University. This led the way for other creative means of teaching and learning through the years.

The board authorized the administration to develop an associate degree in cosmetology, with the classes to be offered in a temporary mobile unit located between Instruction East and Instruction West, and the first graduates of the aviation program were announced. Students in the residential construction program built two houses that sold rather quickly.

Instructors Don Stearns and John Pastoor organized a charter bus trip to Stratford, Ontario to attend a Shakespeare play in the fall of 1974. The $16 cost covered the price of both the bus ride and ticket to the performance. This was the first trip of what has become an annual field trip sponsored by MCC. The college also held a Snow Festival during the last week in February of 1975, and Betty Albert of Belding was named Snow Queen. Activities included snow sculpting and a smurfing contest (from the Smurfs TV show).

10th Anniversary

The year 1975 marked the 10th anniversary of the founding of the college, and a birthday party was celebrated on March 2 in the learning resource center in the Administration Building. Lois Springsteen coordinated the festivities. College family and community members attended the celebration, and recounted the successes of the past 10 years.

Over those years, college salaries increased significantly. By 1975 the following salaries were recorded:

Business manager, $17,200.
Vocational dean, $19,450.
Director of the learning resource center, $18,400.
President, $28,500.

Ground was broken on May 30 for construction of the Activities Building. A news release from MCC reported:

> As the first ground was being broken for the Community College Activities Building, MCC President Dr. Clifford J. Bedore stated "during nine years of dreaming, wishing and planning for this building, progress seemed slow, obstacles seemed insurmountable, and hopes rose and fell, but the commitment to the need was maintained." The new facility, scheduled for use by fall 1976, is designed for student activities, food services, music instruction, large group gatherings and physical education activities.
>
> Included in the plan is a swimming pool, the only indoor pool in the district. It is expected that the pool will not only serve the physical education needs of MCC students, but will also be used by area schools, senior citizens, and other interested adults. Dr. Bedore concluded his comments by saying, "this building should be another link in our attempts to make the community a real part of Montcalm Community College."
>
> Construction is being handled by Pioneer Construction of Grand Rapids, Van's Plumbing and Heating of Cedar Spring, and Power's Electric from Grand Rapids. Kitchen equipment will be installed by Steger-Shewel Company of Toledo, Ohio. (Springsteen, 1975)

But not all was well as financial challenges continued. Due to those challenges, the board voted to eliminate the aviation program, eliminate one teaching position in the auto mechanics program, and reduce the science faculty to two full-time positions. Just a couple months later, state auditors informed the college that MCC owed the state $105,000 because the college constructed a vocational building with state funds rather than a classroom building "as promised" (MCC board minutes). President Bedore denied this claim.

In the summer of 1975, the college launched an associate degree in General studies. Stearns, a member of the science faculty, was employed to plan programs for the forthcoming Activities Building, and a float designed and manned by MCC students won first prize in Greenville's Danish Festival Parade.

Buildings on campus were given their new, official names: the Library/Administration Building, the Instruction East Building, the Instruction West Building, the Vocational/Technical Building, and the Activities Building (under construction). The Veterans' Club constructed a football field on campus, and six teams began a flag football intramural season, with the faculty fielding one of the six teams. The basketball team embarked on a 27-game schedule, with Bob Oosdyke as coach. The board set student admission prices for interscholastic athletic events at 50 cents.

Celebrating America's Bicentennial

As the nation's bicentennial year began in 1976, MCC made plans for its own celebration of the nation's history. Sally Morais, who served as academic secretary, registrar and admissions director from 1972 to 2001, remembers well the special celebrations. "We held a bicentennial fashion show, and I participated! Our celebration included a community picnic, with tents set up for community members of all ages. We even had kids' activities like sack races, and a hot air balloon demonstration" (Morais, 2013).

Three students; Candy Jorgenson, 19, Grant Elliot, 23, and Judy Carpenter, 36; put together a time capsule to be sealed and opened during MCC's 25th anniversary. The capsule contained Kodak slides of the new construction in progress on campus, the bicentennial celebration, college catalogs and newsletters, and photographs of classes and events. It also contained a cassette recording with the following message:

This week is April 26 through April 30, 1976. MCC is joining together with the rest of the nation in celebrating the 200th anniversary of our country. This time capsule is part of that celebration. It is our attempt to share with you our feelings and spirit of this celebration. We thought you might enjoy comparing your experiences in your time with our experiences of the past. We've also included, for your enjoyment, a tape recording of some of the music popular in our day.

Because our students vary in backgrounds and age, a feeling of warmth and friendship prevails on campus. Some students drive distances of 40 to 50 miles, while others live very close to campus. Some of us have gone directly from high school to college, while others of us have been out of school for a long time and are just now able to attend college.

We would like to suggest that this time capsule be perpetuated, with some of you adding mementos of your time, and passing them on to future MCC generations. We hope some mementos will be included during the 25th anniversary year that can be preserved in a capsule and opened on the 50th anniversary of MCC.

We'd like to express our appreciation to the administration, and especially to Mrs. Lois Springsteen and Mr. Charles Tetzlov, for their support, assistance, and contributed items. This time capsule is dedicated to you in the future, from us in the past. (Elliot cassette recording, 1976)

1976 Time Capsule Contents

1. The Bicentennial Flag that was flown over Montcalm Community College from April 26, 1976, through July 4, 1976, purchased by Springsteen.
2. 1976 Montcalm Community College (advertising) flyer.
3. *Daily News* & *Belding Banner* newspaper dated March 4, 1976.

4. Four color copies of "Events of the Day'" (Mon-Thurs) dated April 26, 27, 28, and 29th 1976.
5. The Schedule of Events for "American Festival" that took place the week of April 26, 1976.
6. The list from Commencement for the years 1973, 1974, 1975, and 1976.
7. One Bicentennial Quarter (taped underneath lid).
8. Handmade history folder with photos from 1976 (cover page) Aerial View.
9. 2 Cassette tapes (selected songs of the 70s, and conversation with the three student compilers).
10. *27C*, a book of writings from the Montcalm Community College, 1975 Creative Writing Class.
11. Two photos of the Montcalm Community College "Marathon Men" (*Guinness Book* record holders).
12. Thank-You card to Burns from the Marathon Men.
13. A certificate from the State Senate Resolution No. 431 honoring the participants in the Montcalm Community College Basketball Marathon, dated May 6, 1976.
14. Two cases each containing 24 individual Kodak photographic slides.
15. Six individual slides from May 1976.
16. Seven Montcalm Community College Catalogs, 66/67, 67/68, 70/71, 73/74, 74/75, 75/76, 76,77
17. Twenty-seven 5 x 7 black and white photos

This time capsule was kept in the vault in the basement of the Administration Building and was not opened until the 25th anniversary, and the items have been retained in the college library. New items, including a copy of *Montcalm Community College – Creating Futures Then, Now, Always* and the interview videos produced as part of this project, will be included, with a directive to open and add to during the college's 75th and 100th anniversaries.

During the bicentennial year, the college also further cultivated its relationships with state and local organizations. It hosted the regular meeting of the Michigan Community College Association, and also entered into an agreement with the Community Players of Montcalm, Inc., for a 10-month use of the Barn Theater for community performances and rehearsals. With the renovations completed in the Barn Theater, the MCC drama students inaugurated the new season by presenting three one-act plays in the refurbished facility. Further improvements to the Barn Theater were soon authorized, including the construction of a new patio for $490.

Social Science Instructor Morford was named to receive the 1976 Master Teacher Award, which would in the future become known as the Leslie K. Morford Faculty Recognition Award. Morford was commended for his enthusiasm for both his academic discipline and his students, as well as his personable and creative style of delivering instruction and engaging his students.

During the summer of 1976, MCC trustees passed a resolution to "encourage efforts toward the goal of establishing an Area Vocational Center," but sent a letter to the Montcalm Area Intermediate School District indicating that it would not be interested in being the operating agency for the proposed center (MCC board minutes). The college also began the paving of the two parking lots west of the Library/Administration Building, and building a softball field on the west side of the campus.

Activities Building Opens

By August, the new Activities Building was complete and ready for use, including the new swimming pool. The following news release was prepared by Springsteen, administrative assistant to the president:

> The Montcalm Community College natatorium (pool) is ready for use. Several credit classes have been developed as well as special non-credit swim instruction. Open swimming for the public begins Wednesday, September 1. Hours reserved for the general public to use the pool for recreational swimming are from 8-10 p.m. Monday, Wednesday, Thursday and Friday,

and 9-10 p.m. Tuesdays. There is no age limitation. An admission fee of 35 cents per person per swim will be charged, or season (semester) tickets are available at the rate of $8 for an individual, $20 for family of three and $5 for each additional family member up to six members.

Tiny Tot Swimming is scheduled for Mondays and Wednesdays from 9-10 a.m. for preschoolers. A rate of 50 cents a class will be charged for all swimming instruction. Other special instruction will be held Wednesday, Thursday and Friday from 6-7 p.m. for children 5-15. This class will be grouped according to swimming ability with students receiving a certification card from the American Red Cross if he or she has satisfactorily passed required skills. Adult swimming instruction will be offered Wednesday, Thursday, and Friday from 7-8 p.m. for persons 16 years and older. Special instruction classes will be conducted for eight weeks beginning September 8.

A one credit hour advanced lifesaving class (PE133) has been recently developed and added to the schedule. It will be conducted Thursdays from 2-4 p.m. for 14 weeks beginning September 16. (Springsteen, 1976)

Developmental Education

Dan Snook was hired part time in 1976 to create the developmental education program. He held a bachelor's degree in education and a master's degree in reading improvement from Central Michigan University, and taught at Central Montcalm High School following his graduate studies. During the summer of 1976, Burns contacted CMU to ask if they had anyone they could recommend in reading improvement. Their reply was, "You have this guy right down the road." With this information, Burns contacted Snook. Mulder worked that summer designing the program. The emphasis was just on reading at first, with writing and math added later.

Prior to this time, English Instructor Blake had two small rooms in the one-story classroom building with special reading machines that he had purchased so students could use self-paced technology as a non-credit assist to help improve their reading skills. There were no student assessment or placement tests prior to this time, nor was there any method of screening students, except for the recommendations of the counselors. The first testing program to be used was called Revrac, named after its creator, Carver, spelled backwards. It was quick, inexpensive, and easily scored on carbon copies. Students lined up in the lower level of the Administration Building to take these early tests. Jeff Morris was hired for the first year as a part-time tutor to assist Snook, and also taught in COPE.

Montcalm Area Career Center

As the activities building began its busy schedule, plans for the proposed skills center moved forward as well. The MCC board deeded 10 acres of land to the MAISD on which to construct the proposed building. By January 1977, the MAISD received $2.6 million to construct the Montcalm Area Career Center on the corner of MCC's campus.

Tragedy Strikes Again

Another horrible tragedy occurred on May 2, 1977, when an MCC faculty member was brutally murdered. Gerald H. (Jerry) Freid was a social science instructor who lived at Heritage Hill in Grand Rapids. He was a bachelor and lived alone, but he had a fairly strong guard dog. When his girlfriend was unable to reach him by phone, she called the police. Officers had a difficult time getting in the house because of the dog. When they did, they found Freid badly beaten. He died three days later. Detective Robinson, also an MCC student, came to the college campus and searched through record books to see if there were any disgruntled students, but there were none. For years, police were unsuccessful in solving the crime. Four years later a cold case detective asked himself how the perpetrator got into the house with the dog. There had been no evidence of the dog being tranquilized. He surmised that a dog trainer could have entered successfully. Interestingly, he was able to track down a dog-trainer in the Jackson State Prison who was serving time for a similar crime. His name was Philip Ricardo Hayes. He confessed. It was a robbery. Hayes later passed away while in prison (Edwards).

Campus Life Continues

Kenric DeLong was hired in 1977 as full-time social science instructor to take Freid's place. It was DeLong who made the recommendation to the administration that the Master Teacher Award be named for Morford.

Focus on academics resumed, and there was additional emphasis on expanding course offerings to reach a broader audience. Pat Willison joined the staff as director of continuing education. Classes for busy adults in such areas as health, fitness, recreation, safety, and personal and professional development were soon offered to the larger community, in addition to special events and activities.

Also in April 1977, Bedore announced his retirement as president, effective June 30, 1978. The board approved a timetable for the selection of a new candidate, and set the salary range for the new leader at $30,000 to $40,000. By November, trustees narrowed the number of candidates for president to six, and invited four of them for on-campus interviews. In February, the board selected Dr. Herbert Stoutenburg as the new president.

During the last year before his retirement, Bedore led the college through the construction of a gravel surfaced parking lot west of the Activities Building, proposed lighting for parking lot B, and encouraged the acceptance of a budget of $6,000 for the exploration of a developmental reading program as proposed by Dean Burns. He also supported the creation of an arboretum as an annex to the Instruction East Building. And at this point in the school's history, he led a college of 14 administrators, three counselors, 26 full-time instructors, and 20 non-classified staff members.

The 10th annual MCC commencement was conducted in May 1978 for 192 graduates, and a retirement dinner was held to honor Bedore for his years of faithful service to the college. In an article published in Greenville's *The Daily News*, John Stafford later wrote:

When Bedore became president, the college was caught up in the same sort of student unrest that raged on most other campuses during the Vietnam years. A calm and steady sort of individual, Bedore buttoned down the hatches and MCC chopped wood until the war years' storm passed. He proved a very stabilizing force and brought a feeling of order back to the college.

Visible on the campus most of the time, Bedore kept the college in good light. And near the end of his term, a beautiful new activities building was completed." (Stafford, 1978)

Bedore was thankful that he did not have the challenges of being the first president, but he still faced some of the county factions that Fink had experienced earlier. These, however, seemed to mellow during his tenure. Bedore was pleased when Stoutenburg was chosen as his successor, and believed he would successfully move the college forward. Indeed, Stoutenburg would bring a rich academic background to his new post.

Top: Dr. Clifford Bedore served as MCC's business manager before becoming president. Bottom: MCC's special activities day, known as Day on the Grass, featured a tug of war.

Top: Librarian John Carlson in the auto shop with Instructor Dick Fox;
Bottom: Auto program students work on a block-boring machine, used to
increase the diameter of cylinders in a motor block.

These planes on MCC's campus were used in the
aviation power mechanics program in the 1970s.

Jesse Fox served as an aviation power mechanics instructor
and dean of vocational and technical studies.

Dr. Donald Burns joined MCC's staff as a counselor
in the student services department.

Top: MCC celebrated its 10th anniversary on March 2, 1975.
Bottom: Construction began in 1975 on the Activities Building.

Top: Grant Elliot, Judy Carpenter and Candy Jorgensen assembled a time-capsule in 1976 to be opened during MCC's 25th anniversary celebration.
Bottom: MCC's bicentennial celebration in 1976

Top: Dennis Mulder instructs a humanities class.
Bottom: Nancy Fox instructs an art student.

Chapter 3

Academic Development

According to Lois Springsteen, this new era of the school's history is best recognized as a time of "academic development" and "entering the computer age" (Springsteen interview, 2014).

Third President Installed

On July 1, 1978, Dr. Herbert N. Stoutenburg assumed the MCC presidency. The *Howard City Record* reported:

> Most of Dr. Herbert N. Stoutenburg's collegiate and professional life has been directed toward education.
>
> After attending Flint Junior College, he graduated from Michigan State College in 1947 with a BS degree in business administration. He received an MA degree from MSU in 1953, majoring in general education administration. In 1968, Dr. Stoutenburg earned his doctor of education degree, also from Michigan State.
>
> From 1947-48, Dr. Stoutenburg worked as a member of an auditing team with Ernst and Ernst Public Accountants.
>
> Between 1948 and 1958 he was employed by Michigan State University, the first eight years as assistant to the registrar; then as an executive officer directing

administrative functions of the MSU Vietnam advisory groups in South Vietnam; followed by a shorter period of time as administrative assistant to the registrar in 1958.

In 1959, Dr. Stoutenburg became director of admissions and registrar for Oakland University at Rochester, Michigan. In 1965 he became Oakland's assistant president for administration following a one-year position as dean of student affairs.

He became President at Alpena Community College in 1971 and in 1976 accepted the position of assistant secretary for the Lansing-based Michigan Community College Association.

To honor Stoutenburg and welcome him to the community as the new MCC president, several open houses were held throughout the county in various locations. Community members expressed a general sense of optimism and expectancy regarding the future of the college and the role it would play in the days ahead.

Challenges, Opportunities, and Key Players

There were some immediate challenges the new president had to tackle. Some conflicts and disagreements developed between the college and the Community Players, a local drama group, regarding the use of the Barn Theater. After several appearances before the board, these matters were placed in the hands of the administration to resolve. The college was also concerned with the poor condition of Sidney Road, and asked Stoutenburg to contact the county and express those concerns.

New programs were also being developed. The newly established developmental learning skills program needed a full-time leader, and Dan Snook was selected to fill that role as a member of the full-time faculty. He would hold that role for more than 25 years. The program provided one-on-one instruction for students needing remediation in reading, writing and math. Credit courses were also soon created in efficient study and related topics. The academic department was labelled Student Development and SD was assigned as the prefix to course numbers. "The curriculum included three to four one-credit-hour courses in reading, then math. The taking of these courses was purely voluntary. If a student tested low, he or she was invited to enroll in these courses" (Snook, 2014). Snook was happy to report that success rates in freshmen English and elementary algebra significantly improved for those who engaged in the developmental courses. "We found that those who took our courses and passed them did as well as those who originally got a clean bill of health. Those who did not take them, did not do as well" (Snook).

During the 1979 spring semester, the college established its official colors as green and yellow. Board deliberations included the authorization to spend up to $16,000 to remodel a room in the Activities Building to accommodate the transfer of the bookstore from the Administration Building, which was completed in August 1979. The board also authorized the designation for Clifford Bedore as president emeritus, a salary figure of $35,310 for President Stoutenburg, and a final budget for the upcoming year as $1,933,562.

During the beginning of the Stoutenburg era, tuition rates were set at $14 for resident students, up from $13, $21 for non-residents, up from $19, and $32 for out-of-state students, up from $30. The wages for part-time instructors were set at $251 per credit hour with mileage to be paid for travel to and from class starting with the 31st mile per trip.

Happily, college officials announced that the fall 1979 enrollment was "the highest ever" in MCC's history, and had the highest number of credit hours as well (MCC board minutes). Faculty members were pleased with a new faculty lounge in the Activities Building, and board members appreciated the improvements and resurfacing of Sidney Road.

Jane LaLonde was hired as secretary to the directors of nursing and occupational education, and would serve the college as an administrative assistant until 2012. She became an information hub of the college, and a key facilitator of academic operations.

The spring semester saw another record enrollment in the history of the college, as the campus celebrated its 15th anniversary. Burns was named vice president, and TV comedian George Gobel appeared at MCC, sponsored by the Sheridan VFW Post.

As the music and drama departments continued to develop, Jane Karlsen of Greenville was assigned to direct the MCC choir and vocal groups, while Kenneth Smith continued to direct the jazz band. Students in an EightCAP, Inc., program completed a restoration and remodeling of the Barn Theater that included creation of dressing rooms and restrooms. Several programs were scheduled for the academic year, arranged by MCC's community services department.

Curricula also continued to expand with the allocation of $2,700 to plan and establish an associate degree in nursing (RN) program. MCC received permission to begin the new nursing program in January 1981. To help generate funds for additional faculty and expenses, the board voted to hold a millage election on March 31, 1981, to ask voters for .75 mills for operation. The millage election, however, was not successful. The board set a date of October 27, 1981, to again ask voters for an increase of .75 mills for operation, but later decided to postpone the holding of another millage, due to some scheduling issues.

In April of 1981, Karen Carbonelli was selected by the board to fill a vacancy left by the resignation of Trustee Einer Thorlund, Jr. and was officially elected in June along with Orville Trebian, for whom the current Orville and Dorothy Trebian Conference Room in the Donald C. Burns Administration/Library Building is named, and Eric Halvorsen. Carbonelli would later become board chair and prove to be an invaluable addition to MCC's leadership for years to come. As of 2015, she continues in the chair role, and is in her 34th year as a trustee. "I was so pleased to have the opportunity to join the MCC board. Herb Stoutenburg was the president, and I knew him quite well. He was a fine gentleman," Carbonelli reflects. "Funding was quite an issue when I arrived, and he did an excellent job pulling things together. He was considered heavy-handed by some, but did what had to be done. Bea Doser was also a wonderful individual, and an excellent chair" (Carbonelli, 2014).

MCC Foundation

Stoutenburg announced final approval for the establishment of the MCC Foundation with Ash serving as its first president. The MCCF "became the philanthropic arm of the college, to encourage and financially support the mission of creating a learning community" (Terry Smith, 2014). Founded in 1981 as a 501c3 organization, the Foundation would see steady fund growth, and the active participation of highly engaged directors from the community. The original directors included Ash (president), Ellen Baker (vice president), Stanley Chase, Kenneth Lehman, Homer Miel, Trebian, and Stoutenburg (secretary/treasurer).

Ash is known to have made the statement to Burns, "The first million is the toughest to raise. The rest will come more easily" (T. Smith, 2014).

New Highs and Lows

Despite the support of the newly established foundation, the college faced some financial challenges. Adjustments were made.

The first students in the new MCC associate degree in nursing program began classes during the fall of 1981. That semester also saw the groundbreaking ceremonies for construction of the proposed greenhouse to be attached to the Instruction East Building.

Despite the financial cloud hanging over the institution, 226 students received degrees or certificates at the 15th annual commencement, and Science Instructor Don Stearns was selected to study in Russia in recognition of his efforts and contributions to the advancement of physical education in Montcalm County.

Good fortune emerged as the district voters approved an increase in the operating millage of .75 mills for MCC by a vote of 2,646 to 1,758. The millage was levied for the next five years. Because of this, the pool would soon be able to reopen as it was closed due to financial constraints for nearly a year. The board also adopted a revised 1982-83 budget of $2,756,000 as a result of the successful millage vote.

Entering the Computer Age

As the world of education moved into the computer age, MCC's interest in purchasing a computer and creating classes in data processing emerged. Thankfully, a donor provided $6,800 for the purchase of a Model 34 IBM computer, and Earl (Chris) Christensen was employed as the first data processing instructor. According to Burns, Christensen did an amazing job of bringing MCC into the computer age, and laying the foundation for its information technology programs for years to come (Burns interview).

Sally Morais served as registrar at the time, and reflects on what it was like when MCC entered into the age of technology:

Montcalm Community College began the first steps in computerization in the 1980s. The first attempt was processing report cards. Prior to this, staff typed up report cards for all students prior to the end of the semester. We typed name, address, semester, year, each course name and number and credit hours. When grades were submitted to the records office they were handwritten on the report cards and then semester and accumulated grade point averages were figured on calculators. One copy was mailed to the student and one copy was filed in the student's file after transcripts were all typed, also each done individually.

I can't remember the name of the company we hired to process these report cards but it was two gentlemen in Lansing, who later moved their company to a marina in Muskegon, where they lived on a boat! When the report cards came to us the first time, nearly all of them were incorrect and had to be re-done by hand. We didn't use this company for very long.

The next step was to get registration computerized. Our old process involved filling out hundreds of class cards prior to registration. We hand wrote the course number, code or section number, and credit hours. These were lined up in order in long, narrow boxes. When a section was empty, the class was full. We kept hash marks for each class on a sheet so that we had a number when instructors wanted to know how many were in a class. After we were fully computerized, Les Morford still always came looking for the hash mark sheet! Students had to fill out one program directory form and a card for each class for which they registered. It was a rather lengthy process for them.

When registration ended, class lists were typed up for each class and distributed to instructors. Final official rosters were then typed up at the end of the drop/add period and distributed, signed by the instructors and returned to records to be used as official counts for state and federal records. There were times we had to hunt down instructors to get these rosters back. Auditors frowned if we didn't have them.

Mid-semester rosters were also typed up and distributed to faculty to note any problems so that we could follow up with students that weren't attending or perhaps needed some counseling or help.

Finally, we typed up final grade sheets for faculty to write in final grades. Then the process of filling out report cards began again.

I can't remember the name of the young lady that worked with me to begin the computerization of registration but she was very good at what she did and I really liked working with her. I think the computer we were using was an IBM System 36. This young lady, however, was soon offered a job with IBM and left MCC. A very young man took over. He seemed to me very shy and I was skeptical at first about working with him. But he proved to be a great guy to work with – thank you Rod Middleton! He was very patient and helpful through the whole, stressful (for me) process and we soon had everything up and running. Several years later Darcella Daws was added to the technology staff and she was also great to work with.

So registration, class lists, and report cards eventually became as easy as putting forms in a printer and pushing a few buttons. We would later often laugh about the old ways of doing these things and how much time the processes took. But we had fun doing them, working together and double checking to make sure grades and GPAs were correct before sending them out to students.

There were many changes in computer programs over the years, each with their own positives and headaches. It was an interesting, often fun, often frustrating, time in my career at MCC and I'm very glad to have been a part of it. (Morais)

At the same time computers arrived at MCC, the student senate used student activities fees to purchase and install a TV projection screen, a 10-foot down-link TV satellite dish, a tape deck and laser disc player.

Santa's Super Sunday

The first Santa's Super Sunday was launched by Pat Willison in December 1982, with Santa on campus meeting hosts of area children with a gift and a smile. Many members of the community came to MCC's campus for the first time, and expressed gratitude for the school's hospitality. The initial idea was born to create an event that would thank the community for their support of the successful millage campaign. Willison shares, "At first I was thinking of just having a free swim day in the MCC pool. But since it was around holiday time, I decided to add a visit with Santa - something children could do while waiting for a swim" (Willison, October 20, 2014). She continues,

"Then we solicited cookies from Leppink's and orange drink from McDonald's and Burger King, hoping we hadn't overestimated when we asked for enough to serve 400 people. That first year we estimated there were 1,000 visitors. We totally ran out of refreshments after the first of three hours." (Willison)

Carbonelli reflects, "I believe the community is a far better place because of the college." One of the examples she cites is Santa's Super

Sunday. "I was not totally sure about the idea at first, but when I saw all the families coming to campus, I knew it was a great idea. It introduced many of the community to our college, while also brightening their holidays. I knew that many children never had their picture taken with Santa, so I bought a Polaroid camera to take photos of them. I could tell we made a difference" (Carbonelli).

New Challenges and Controversy

Yet, with all the good fortune and financial progress, MCC still found itself facing several financial challenges. By April of 1983, the decision was made to drop the aviation program due to costs and declining program enrollments. The college held an auction of airplanes, parts and machinery for more than 300 aviation enthusiasts. MCC raised $149,000 from the auction.

Members of the MCC faculty, along with representatives of K-12 faculties from area schools, attended the April board meeting to express their dismay at the failure to reach resolution on a master agreement, which expired in August 1982. Later in May, members of the Faculty Council engaged in "informational picketing" at the campus entrance to protest failure to reach an agreement. Finally, following a year of negotiations, the Faculty Council and the board agreed to a master agreement, retroactive to August 1982.

The year weighed heavily on Stoutenburg, however, and in June 1983 he announced his intended retirement effective on June 30, 1984. The board selected Burns, currently serving as the college's vice president, to be the new president.

But controversy continued. Retroactive pay increases were given to the business manager, vice president, director of personnel, and two members of the support staff. The MCC Faculty Council expressed "outrage" (MCC board minutes).

The Daily News editorially stated that the MCC board "abused the voters" for granting pay raises to four administrators and two secretaries after stating they would not do so when seeking additional millage. The board defended its actions, however, explaining that the salary increases were not being paid with new millage money, but with previously existing funds. According to Morford, the board claimed to have used the millage money (new money) to repair the roof on the Administration/Library Building. This became known as the "old money/new money controversy" (Morford). "Until this time, the college had been relatively free of any major controversy" (Morford).

On July 1, 1984, Stoutenburg retired from the presidency of MCC and Burns assumed the position. The following month, Stoutenburg was named president emeritus. Reflecting on his time at MCC, Stafford wrote in *The Daily News:*

> When Dr. Stoutenburg arrived in 1978, the college once again had a good match. An experienced community college administrator, Stoutenburg also was a promoter and he took the college's story and programs off campus and into the district at a time when this was needed. The result of his steady, always positive, aggressive leadership showed when a request for more college millage was approved by a substantial margin in 1982. (Stafford)

In a similar vein, Reporter Terence Smith mused:

> Although Stoutenburg's tenure has enjoyed the benefits of joining the college after its infant years, there have still been some problems, particularly during his early years, when the faltering economy had an impact.
>
> "Our greatest problem was a problem of money for us," he said, adding "the college had to borrow against anticipated taxes for three years."

In 1982 however, voters in all Montcalm County school districts except Tri County and Lakeview, approved the college request for .75 mill for five years.

Stoutenburg was elated, calling the win, "a great victory for the people of the Montcalm Community College district ...

"I guess we pulled the county together and came up with a 60-40 (percent) split in favor of the millage," Stoutenburg said. "We have a lot of great support."

"I think we're just getting ready for a great breakthrough," he added.

Part of that community acceptance was the work conducted by Dean of Community Services Don Burns. During Stoutenburg's term, the public had more access to the college.

"It literally took us years to establish the community service functions," Burns said.

"I think Don (Burns) is going to be a good president," Stoutenburg said. Don's got a staff that he can really work with."

The community college has matured. (Terence Smith)

Top: Dr. Herbert Stoutenburg served as MCC's third president. Bottom: MCC entered the computer age in the early 1980s with a Model 34 IBM Computer.

Top: Vernon Blake (at the piano) and Ken Smith (in white) perform with the MCC Jazz Band in the early 1980s. Bottom: Blake also worked with the MCC choir. Both performances were held in the Instruction West Auditorium.

Stanley Ash, first chair of the MCC Board of Trustees, first president of the MCC Foundation, donor, friend, and pillar of MCC and the entire Montcalm community

MCC's Santa's Super Sunday was
first conducted in 1982.

Top: MCC's Panhandle Area Center under construction; Bottom: Dr. Donald Burns leads the ribbon cutting ceremony at the opening of the Panhandle Area Center in Howard City.

Chapter 4

---◆-◆-◆---

Cultivating Relationships
and Partnerships

D on Burns was raised on a farm near Carson City, and knew the greater Montcalm community well. He attended St. Mary's Catholic School and Carson City High School. Later, he earned his BA degree in accounting from Aquinas College in Grand Rapids, his master's degree in school counseling and his doctorate in higher education administration from Michigan State University.

Fourth President Emerges from MCC Leadership

Burns first came to MCC in 1971 as a counselor, and was assigned the special project of developing an area guidance center, which he cultivated for three years. He was named dean of students in 1974, and dean of students and community services in 1976, before assuming the role of vice president.

As a family man and one who constantly aspired for balance in his life, Burns enjoyed a close relationship with his wife, Maureen, and four children. Maureen Burns was active in the community as a motivational and inspirational speaker, author, and humorist. She later took on the roles of weekly columnist for *The Daily News* and founded One Book One County Montcalm.

Burns loved to jog, read historical fiction, and travel abroad.

He reflects, "When Herb Stoutenburg arrived in 1978, part

of what he saw at MCC was the need to move from a passive institution to an active one, and he restructured the business plan of the college. He accomplished several major goals" (Burns). He continues to explain some of those accomplishments as "realigning the curriculum, eliminating programs that weren't carrying themselves, and focusing more on the training and instructional needs expressed by the community" (Burns). "He also began some new programs like data processing, led us through a successful millage election, and established the MCC Foundation." Burns was pleased with the additional infrastructure that Stoutenburg provided for the college, and was eager to build on that.

Burns became president in 1984 and had already been at MCC for 13 years. He had significant knowledge of the college and what was needed. He itemized these as:

> 1. A way to solve our conflicts (we were tiring ourselves out with internal strife). We needed something like mutual gains to move us forward.
> 2. A way to more effectively take the college to the community. We were still to some degree a junior college and needed a greater connection to the community.
> 3. A clarification of roles. We had a lot of sincere people, but needed specific clarification on what each should be doing.

In 1985, MCC began a new bargaining contract. The faculty leadership and Burns received training from a group in New Jersey, based on a book titled *Getting to Yes*. It taught a concept of mutual gains and interest-based bargaining in an organized, civilized, and data-based fashion. "We learned this could be done," Burns states, "although it is never easy. The faculty association was founded in the 1960s, and some of the support staff had organized in the early 1980s, as well as the administration. By 1984, everyone was organized. Not everyone needed to like how the new concept worked, but at least know how it worked" (Burns). Through this experience, the MCC leadership also learned the importance of training in the process, and has continued to incorporate the training before going to the table ever since. "Don't mumble through it on your own," Burns cautions. "Train each time you do it. The mutual gains concept is an unnatural act among consenting adults and, thus, you need training in problem-solving and cooperation. But it can't happen without the participation and inclusion of all parties." (Burns interview).

Establishing Connections

Another item that Burns believed he needed to address early in his administration was better connection between staff, faculty and administration. Burns explains, "We had connected well with students, but lacked connection between departments. We still needed to become like a family. We also needed a stronger connection between the community and board" (Burns). He believes the institution did a good job cultivating this over time. The centers in Howard City, Ionia, and Greenville became meaningful connections with the community. Also, the board sometimes met on campus, but also began to meet in the communities throughout the seven school districts. Soon, the board met routinely in those settings. "When we would go there, like Carson City," Burns explains, "we would not talk about the college. The intention was to ask, 'What is happening in Carson City?' They would share neat things they were doing and proud of, and challenges they faced. This became a built-in environmental scanning piece" (Burns). The trustees kept a list of where they were meeting individually as well, along with the organizations to which they belonged. Soon, the staff did the same. With time, all the members of the MCC family came to understand that they were the college, and continued to connect more effectively between students, staff, and community.

Burns also saw the need to restructure MCC's governance. "We were traditional," he declares, "but moved toward policy governance." With time, agreed upon and communicated policies drove decisions rather than individual administrators. The administration sought a role of serving, supporting and enabling. For example, more and more, faculty peers evaluated instructors rather than administrators doing all of the evaluation. Burns also shares that from 1984 forward, the college had to learn better:

1. How to plan (and how to scan)
2. How to connect
3. How to embrace technology
4. How to enhance faculty development.

"We learned how to better cultivate the three ships of relationship, partnership, and leadership, and also learned how to create trust," Burns added.

Another concern was how to raise friends and funds. For Burns, the cultivation of friends must precede the cultivation of funds. The school needed to learn how to take a fledgling foundation and develop it. Leaders needed to listen and learn from experts. For these reasons, the new leadership used consultants and endeavored to keep learning.

As the school moved forward, it also kept an eye on community development. "We do teaching for the community because we are a community college. We don't do it alone. We learn how to participate in a learning community. We're an important player but not the only player" (Burns).

And since Burns came from the field of counseling, the school's counseling department expanded under his presidency. As early as September 1984, a special needs advocate was employed for students, to make sure students with any special challenges were appropriately accommodated and cared for.

Fresh Opportunities

MCC also received a $144,000 state grant to establish a new small business assistance and training center. Earl (Chris) Christensen was asked to lead the new venture as the school's IT guru. And the board also approved the purchase and construction of a fitness trail at a cost of $5,200.

In an attempt to deliver distance education in a creative venue, the Principles of Economics course was offered via cable TV during the

1985 fall semester, and Rod Nutt was hired as media assistant to help in the production of this course and future distance learning classes.

Administrators, instructors and staff members viewed the official board as visionary, supportive, innovative, and professional in focus. Trustee Karen Carbonelli was named Woman of the Year by the Greenville Business and Professional Women's Organization. Other trustees were also viewed as superior leaders within the greater community, and in touch with the operations of the school. An example of board activity was the establishment of the emeritus status for retired faculty and administrators, and retired member status for retired support staff.

The board also authorized a May 20, 1986 millage election to seek a renewal of the .75 mills for operations previously approved by the voters. It passed by a vote of 1,661 to 336.

In an effort to create an environmentally delightful walkway from the Barn Theater to the main section of the campus, a tree-stump-lined path was installed to connect the Barn Theater with College Drive. It was designated Anderson Lane in honor of the Anderson family who owned the farm prior to the college's acquisition of the property. Signage was placed at the end of the lane.

James Lantz was employed as director of business and finance effective July 14, 1986. Janice Roy was hired as instructor of mathematics and Robert Campbell was employed as instructor of business education, both effective during the 1986 fall semester.

Lantz recalls:

> Ironically, during one of my first days here, Bea Doser came into my office and introduced herself to me, and I didn't know who she was. She was very kind and cordial. That established my impression of Bea over the years, which I certainly maintained. I heard that she was very hands-on during construction, but also very fair, professional, and even-handed. She interacted with employees well.

Crystal the Mastodon

In June 1986, mastodon bones were found on a farm near Crystal. Eventually, these bones would be placed in the care of the University of Michigan and displayed at MCC. The following article was published in *The Daily News* on August 13, 1986:

> SIDNEY – The mastodon bones recently found on the Walter Eldridge property in Crystal Township will be displayed at Montcalm Community College in another year and a half.
>
> Official announcement was made by MCC President Dr. Donald C. Burns at Tuesday's meeting of the Board of Trustees.
>
> Where and how to display the bones is something the college will be thinking about in the coming months.
>
> In a memo to trustees, Burns stated the Eldridges have indirectly donated the relics to MCC through the University of Michigan where cleaning, identification and study is now underway.
>
> The Eldridge donation is made directly to U of M, which will in turn assign them for a permanent loan to MCC. In this arrangement, the university is a sort of "legal guardian" for the specimen in case future cutbacks make it impossible for the college to retain the display, the memo explains.
>
> The university has made display suggestions, and cost to MCC could range from a few thousand dollars to $20,000, Burns said. "The first step," he added, "is to look for a way to display the mastodon without additional building."
>
> Chairman Beatrice Doser indicated she had been told some state funding may be available to help the college. (Walker)

Dr. Daniel Fisher, a paleontologist and assistant curator for the museum of paleontology at the University of Michigan, came to MCC on Wednesday evening, November 19, 1986, to give more information about the mastodon to a gathering of about 65 students and interested spectators who wanted to learn more about the bones.

He gave a brief history of mastodons, explained the methods used to date mastodon bones, and exhibited the bones that were discovered on the Crystal area farm of Walt and Ida Eldridge. He referred to the relic as The Eldridge Mastodon, in honor of the family, but MCC family members referred to it as Crystal, based on the general area where it was discovered.

Fisher explained, "There was a population of about one or two mastodons per square mile in Michigan and theories indicate they became extinct 10,000 years ago … The Eldridge mastodon was a female in its late 20s or early 30s at the time of death, compared to the 55-60 year normal life span of mastodons" (Odette).

President Burns announced that a three-man committee met with Fisher during his visit to discuss various ways to exhibit the bones. He said the timing was right for MCC's acquisition of the bones in over a year from now, since it would not be ready to house it immediately. Burns also explained that with the major growth and expansion projects the college was currently experiencing, it will be more than ready for the bones when they arrive.

Interestingly, Burns also said, "the display will provide an educational advantage to young people who can come to the 20-year-old college and enjoy the new sesquicentennial display featuring 100-year-old buildings and ponder the 10,000-year-old bones" (Odette).

He was referring to a one-room schoolhouse that had just been moved to the campus, and a one-hundred year-old log house that was in the process of being dismantled and reassembled at the college. These were the early buildings of what would become Heritage Village.

Heritage Village

It was during this 20th year of the campus, 1986, that a new concept emerged – the formation of an historic village on the college property. The birth of this idea cannot be credited to any one individual, but by a confluence of interests that remarkably took hold at the same time.

Yet, everyone who had a part in those early roots had one desire in common – to preserve the heritage of the past as a learning tool for the future. For this reason, it is most appropriate that the name given to this creative venue would come to be Heritage Village. The story of Heritage Village is a fascinating one with a humble beginning, an evolving vision, and the amazing dedication of volunteer thinkers, movers, shakers, and workers. It was birthed on the MCC campus in 1986, and has maintained a symbiotic union ever since. Although it is an independent association, Heritage Village rests on the campus of MCC, and enjoys an active partnership with administrators, faculty members, staff, trustees and students, as well as the community at large.

In the most fascinating confluence of factors, the idea of an historic village on the campus of MCC emerged as: 1.) Four women: Rosemary Long, Maxine Harris, Mildred Mahan, and Hazel Smith, traveled to Ludington to visit the Historic White Pine Village. When they returned, they thought they could copy the idea and this would be a wonderful addition to MCC's campus. 2.) The Shoen family of Crystal was hoping to preserve the heritage of its family log house, and explored the possibility of MCC's interest in acquiring it. 3.) Dr. William Seiter, MAISD superintendent, belonged to an organization seeking a way to preserve a one-room schoolhouse as an historical/educational tool for future generations. 4.) The state of Michigan was looking for creative ways to celebrate its upcoming sesquicentennial and local committee members sought a unique way to do that in Montcalm County.

The Shoen Log House

In the summer of 1986, the Shoen family of nearby Crystal approached MCC's President Burns with an offer (first discussed as early as the 1979/80 school year) to donate its family log cabin constructed in 1860 to become an historic fixture on the college property. The Shoen siblings explained that it belonged to their parents, and was the home that carried their childhood memories. Burns recalls:

> The family contacted me and wanted to give the
> log building. My understanding was that it was a barn.

Quite frankly, I didn't 'get it.' But it's a wonderful example of the community's participation of community relationship with the college. Hazel Smith was very excited about the idea of capturing history, and she and others had this amazing imagination. She was just a community member – that is to say, not a member of the college. That's the beauty of this. It was from the grassroots of the community. We align with and enhance the community and community activities. It develops as it should when you are open to ideas that are beyond what you think from the inside out and this is a great example of that. They saw something that could be a reality — a cultural venue — by capturing pieces of history and bringing them and people together to celebrate our heritage. So the first discussions basically were, 'Here's a building, what do you think?' I was thinking, 'How are we going to take care of this? It's going to just sit out there. What are you going to do with it?' (Burns, 2011)

Despite some of his doubts, Burns went to see the structure as a result of an emergency call. "Please come over here," one of the Shoen family members said strongly over the phone. Burns was told they had to get rid of it and were going to burn it down. The family was pleading, "Please, can't you take it? We really don't want to see it go." So, Burns looked it over. After he saw it, Burns realized it had been a house that was transformed into a barn. He also quickly realized that it couldn't be moved, but rather would have to be taken apart piece by piece and put back together.

After giving this offer some thought, Burns asked Vice President Lantz and Director of Facilities Frank Reeder to visit and examine the log building, situated just west of the town of Crystal. Lantz recalls:

When Frank and I went to look at the Shoen log house, we were surprised to see a fairly good-sized structure with more than one room. It was somewhat of a bi-level structure, with one room as one story, and one section having a room and a half. It was covered by siding over the years, and the area around it was quite overgrown with weeds and brush. We looked around and said, "This is really a neat structure." We did see some rot in some of the logs, but thought, "Okay, if the college wants it, let's do it." (Lantz, 2011)

Reeder was later joined by Jesse Fox and Bill Raymor who spoke with Kenneth Lehman, the owner of Big L Lumber in Sheridan and Greenville and a strong supporter of, and generous donor to the college. Lehman also contributed to the development of the nature trails, which now bear his name. He offered to donate the necessary equipment and personnel to move the log cabin to the west lot at MCC in Sidney. With all this information in hand, Burns asked Fox to make the official arrangements to accept the log house, and proceed with the project.

In preparation for the process of dismantling and moving the structure, Lantz developed a code to mark all of the logs so they could be reassembled properly. Reeder and his custodial staff acquired some little metal tags (bearing a series of letters and numbers) to identify each log, and nailed a tag to each piece. He also crafted a drawing of the structure for the purpose of careful reconstruction. Several MCC employees volunteered to help move the cabin, but those from Big L did most of the work. Lantz again recalls:

Big L got a truck to transport it, and a fork lift to move the logs one by one as the structure was first disassembled, loaded on the truck, brought here, and then put back together. Most of the MCC folks watched. (Lantz, 2011)

At the time, the college had a couple of custodians who had some interest and skill in rebuilding projects -- Gaylerd Cooper, who once served in the Navy's Construction Brigade, and Gary Kieffer, the uncle of today's MCC Information Systems Director Rod Middleton. They were the ones who actually reconstructed the house during the spring of 1987. As they began, they discovered that many of the logs were rotted and not usable. "We had to acquire some logs from a log barn in Sheridan to supplement, but could not get enough to rebuild it exactly the way it was," Lantz explains. Burns talked to the Shoen family about this dilemma, and they felt very disappointed. Their hope was to reconstruct it exactly as it stood in Crystal. But according to Lantz, "There wasn't anything else we could do. So we began to construct it as a one-room log cabin. The logs are a combination of the good logs from the original cabin and some of the good logs from the barn." The second level was therefore eliminated. Local citizen Bill Lacy helped to find replacement logs, and it was Jean Brundage who told them of a barn on Holland Lake Road, north of Sheridan, owned by the Christopherson family, who happily donated the barn for logs. Ed Minion, a member of the MCC maintenance staff at the time, agreed to build a rock foundation, and other volunteers offered to build a new replacement roof.

The reconstruction team also used *chinking* (mortar that lasts) to insert between the logs. Lantz did some searching (primarily in magazines, since the Internet had not yet become widely accessible), and discovered a company in Tennessee called Perma-Chink that developed a product with elastic ability to expand and shrink with the heat and cold. Before applying the Perma-Chinck, the workers drove steel rods down through the logs to keep them in place. The college paid for the chinking, and because the maintenance crew was less busy in the summer, the college allowed Cooper and Kieffer to reconstruct the log house during normal working hours.

Finally, it was completed. To commemorate this event, the college held an open house and invited the Shoen family members as the honored guests. Once they heard Burns' description of the process and arrived on campus to see the reconstructed Shoen Log House for themselves, they were pleased. Mahan was present when the Shoen family made the official presentation to MCC, and remembers how family members gave some interesting facts and stories about how the log house was used (Mahan). A plaque was presented to them as well, which is now located in the log house. It reads, "Montcalm Community College would like to extend a special thank you to Clifford Shoen and his wife Leta, and his sisters, Alta and Velma, for the donation of this historical structure in memory of Barney and Elizabeth Shoen." It also states, "The house stands in Heritage Village as a monument to Montcalm County's early days."

Volunteers set out to fill the cabin with items reminiscent of some of those stories. To furnish it, a rope bed and dresser were donated by Phil Frisbie, who later became the village historian. According to Brundage, Frisbie did a lot of research and work along with his art students at Vestaburg, making quilts, paper-mâché items, crocheted doilies, and woven rugs, and even taught classes on arts and crafts in the log cabin. Frisbie also made hair flowers, and explained how pictures made of the hair of grandparents would be passed down through the generations (Brundage interview).

In a letter dated February 19, 2011, Barney A. Shoen writes, "Although I am too old to remember many of the details, I do remember being reared in that log house. It holds many special memories." Shoen is happy that it is now a part of Heritage Village, and says that the old cabin "speaks for itself." Some of those memories were captured in a newspaper article titled "Area Couples Celebrate 75 Years of Marital Bliss," written by Linda Christensen of *The Daily News* and published on Thursday, January 16, 1997:

> **CRYSTAL** – He was 18 years of age; she 16; he wore a coffee colored suit; she a handmade dress – together they rode from Crystal to Stanton in a Model T-Ford on January 28, 1922, a beautiful, sunny day – their wedding day.
>
> The couple, Clifford and Leta Shoen, lifelong residents of Crystal, will soon be celebrating that special day during their 75th wedding anniversary party with family and friends on January 26.
>
> "I remember the day so well," Leta said, "It was real cold, but beautiful and sunny." The ceremony, which

was short, she said, included a couple of women who worked in the Pastor's office as witnesses. After the ceremony, the couple returned home to a small house next door to the Shoen family farm.

The Shoens eventually expanded their family by having four children, two boys and two girls and later moved into the log cabin which had been built back in 1860. The cabin, which originally sported a second story, is now on display at the Heritage Village in Sidney. (Christensen)

Ilene Thomsen was one of the first volunteers to work in the Shoen Log House, and donated many of the items that are now on display there. She says that when children used to visit the log house, they seemed to always ask the same three questions: Where are the bathrooms? Where is the bedroom? What is the water pail for? Her answers were, "Outside restrooms; the loft was not put in when the cabin was moved; and most everyone drank water from the water pail with a dipper" (Thomsen). Thomsen was also joined by Mahan and Maxine Harris. Maxine writes, "When the children came through, I was one of those who had the fun of explaining the contents and their uses to them. They were so interested and asked so many good questions. They seemed most fascinated by the spinning wheel, feather bed, baby crib, dad's red flannels, old Sears catalogs, button shoes, soap stone (foot heater), kitchen sink, pail-dipper, and rotary towel" (Harris).

Ironically, the Shoen Log House is now Burns' favorite. "My great grandparents had a place like this that I used to see as a youngster. They built it in the 1870s and it was much like this, a wooden building. And now I see the wisdom in acquiring this structure" (Burns).

Kathy Beard serves as today's volunteer in charge of the Shoen Log House. She shares:

> I volunteered to be responsible for the log house when Edna Hansen, who was responsible for it, was unable to continue due to health concerns. That was in

early 2007. Since it was built in 1860, we have many items that were used in the 1860s in the log house that make it interesting to people of all ages to see; sometimes they try to figure out what they were used for. I always tell the children about the chamber pot and get their reaction. I also ask them if they know what the rug beater is, and get all kinds of answers! The most popular answers are fly swatter and something used to spank misbehaving children. I enjoy listening to the older women tell about using some of the things in the cabin when they were younger. (Beard)

The Gaffield School

In between the early discussions of the log house and its reconstruction at MCC, the first building moved to the campus property was actually the one-room schoolhouse. Burns remembers a phone call he received in 1986 from Seiter of the MAISD. Superintendent Seiter asked Burns if he had any interest in obtaining the Gaffield School (located just south of Amble), and offered to help provide some of the money to move it. Constructed in 1904, the school was an excellent example of how one teacher taught all the children from beginners to the eighth grade. It was still furnished with the desks that varied in size from the very tiny to those accommodating taller adolescents.

Seiter writes, "I was a member of MARSP, a formal organization of 'retired' teachers interested in obtaining a one-room school to be maintained as an example of early rural education in Michigan" (Seiter). He continues, "I vividly recall memories of the efforts and energies involved in obtaining and getting the unit moved to Heritage Village."

For Burns, this acquisition made instant sense, since it was educationally related. A decision was quickly made, and the building was donated by its owners at the time, David and Phyllis Larsen. It was moved to its present site in 1986, just before the arrival of the log house project.

Bob Marston, MCC trustee and then-MAISD-counselor, assisted in moving the structure and preparing the site at Heritage Village. He writes, "I worked for the MAISD at the time, and there was a real commitment to helping our area celebrate Michigan's 150th anniversary of becoming a state. Since I was selected as chair for the Sesquicentennial Committee and was also on the board at MCC, I was especially interested in this project. It was the first building to be moved to the campus, and being a school, it made good sense" (Marston).

Brundage, MCC trustee and long-time chair of the Heritage Village Association, remembered how the building was literally moved on a flat-bed truck. She also recalled:

> After moving it here, we added a large, black heating stove that used either wood or coal, and a piano that was a gift of the Baptist church in Crystal. Al Gooding donated the clock on the wall and put pictures on the back wall of actual prior classes at the school. Other items were furnished by retired school teachers. During our first celebration, Eva Main served as our 'teacher,' with a curriculum written by Geraldine Christensen, Eleanor Lentz, and Jean Zimmerman. Phil Frisbie taught the second year, and then Eleanor Lentz became our regular teacher. She was the eldest of 12 children, and actually went to a one-room schoolhouse! Edna Hansen ... was also among the first teachers, and helped with the school. Sharon Ritter continues that custom today, donned in her period costume, and teaches school-age children during the annual Heritage Festival. (Brundage interview)

A flier for the 1987 Heritage Village Celebration at the school read:

> Welcome to our one-room rural school in Heritage Village, Sidney, Michigan. As you enter please step back in time to the 1920s and early 1930s. Let's pretend that Calvin Coolidge is our president. Alexander Groesbeck is our governor. Our flag has 48 stars and we say our pledge differently ...

We hope your visit will be stimulating and interesting. The schoolhouse is not yet completely restored. Our dream is that Heritage Village will grow and be a means of enrichment for our children and a source of joy and refreshment to those for whom it is a "Memory Lane." (Heritage Village, *School Days*)

The structure of the schoolhouse at Heritage Village is somewhat reminiscent of the first schoolhouse constructed in Sidney during 1858, built by volunteers and supervised by the founder of the township, Joshua Noah (Olson, *North Sidney,* 32). Lillian Christophersen shares:

My mother, Alma Corfixsen, was a teacher at the Sidney School (in the 30s, I think). She was instrumental in getting the merry-go-round as the students had nothing to play on. (The swings were put there when I attended in the 40s and early 50s.) When the Township Board was going to take it out of the park, I asked if I could have it. But when they said it was going to Heritage Village, I was happy. It had a warped board on it when I was a kid. We called it "the slippery board" because we could slide off it.

I have given boxes of old school books and supplies that belonged to my mother. I also gave my mother's class picture from County Normal and her old Valentines from the 1930s. (Christophersen)

One of the favorite items in the schoolhouse is an actual photograph of the Gaffield School taken of the students in the academic year of 1915-1916, with teacher Doris Mulholland. It is located on the north wall inside the classroom.

The Heritage Village Association

When the village began, the college was also involved in a grant-funded program called *Montcalm Tomorrow*, intended to be a visioning group to plan the future direction of Montcalm County in all its aspects. Morford served as the executive director while serving on the MCC faculty. Inspired by a vision of what the Shoen Log House and Gaffield School projects could become, several retired individuals in the area began to dream of an entire historic village. Colleagues lovingly and humorously referred to this group as *Montcalm Yesterday!* Hazel Smith, a retired public school teacher from the community, became the first chair of the newly formed association of volunteers, and the official name of Heritage Village was adopted.

In a July 1988 letter, H. Smith wrote, "We believe Heritage Village is an important part of our community, serving as a permanent monument to our history" (H. Smith, official minutes of Heritage Village). A mission statement and a constitution were also drafted by committee members. Their goal was to get other buildings for the village and make it a life-size museum of Montcalm County's heritage. "This organization shall be dedicated to the preservation of the history of the Montcalm County area. In achieving this purpose, the organization will work toward the following specific goals:

- To establish a village where children and adults may learn and enjoy the life of early times.
- To preserve the past by restoring original buildings or replicating original ones.
- To preserve the stories, history and data through written, oral and pictoral histories.
- To conduct an annual Heritage Village Celebration.
- To provide a setting where school children may experience an early classroom.
- To encourage community groups to use and support Heritage Village.
- To promote the village as a historically significant attraction in the county.
- To promote activities that will create and support continued interest in the preservation of the history of the area." (Heritage Village, *Constitution* II:1)

Hazel's son, Peter Smith, developed a concept drawing of what the village could eventually become, including a church, a store, and all the key structures that would have comprised a typical village during the time span of 1860 to 1910. Although this plan was adopted, future acquisitions (including the locomotive, for example) would change the range from 1860 to 1926.

Brundage shared, "Tom Learmont developed a master plan for us, and later contracted a gentleman who did the landscaping at Amway to draft a more detailed drawing, which he did without charge. It was a great big thing that hung in Jesse Fox's garage until we moved it into the depot" (Brundage interview). But it was Fox who designed the original sketch of the future village on October 3, 1986, so that the MCC board would have an idea of the vision before approving it. He writes, "The MCC board wanted some idea of what the finished product would look like before they would approve the idea. This sketch included ideas from several committee members" (Fox letter).

As plans developed and the vision became enlarged, a Native American village was also considered, but that idea was put on hold indefinitely. Since these early beginnings, several other buildings have been added or constructed as re-creations. And while all desired to keep the village as true to life as possible, electricity and running water were later added to accommodate today's needs.

Doser was serving as chair of the MCC board at the time and asked Trustee Brundage to join this committee to represent the college. Brundage started as the first official secretary, then became vice chair, then chair following H. Smith, who faithfully led the committee for its first four years of existence. During this time, the committee had grown to some 20 to 30 individuals from the community, with no other personnel from the college except Terry Smith, who also served as secretary. After Brundage became the chair, she decided to designate people to each building, providing a strong sense of ownership and ongoing creativity. Eleanor Lentz was assigned to the school and Lillian Hansen to the log cabin, followed by Harris, Hansen, and Beard. Brundage steadily chaired the Heritage Village Association until her passing in 2012. Miriam Zimmerman was unanimously elected to become her replacement.

The zealous body of volunteers raised money to acquire and move buildings from across the county to the Heritage Village site, with the understanding that once they were moved, they would become part of the college property. Association volunteers held spaghetti dinners and quilt raffles to raise money for each building, which cost between $10,000 and $20,000 to move! A large part of this sum was paid to the utility companies to take down or hold up power wires as flatbed trucks transported the school, Sidney Township Hall, and others.

Heritage Village Association remains an independent group operating with the college's blessing to promote, celebrate, and expand. Burns explains:

> As it emerged over the years, it continued to be a wonderful example of the relationship between the community and the college and community ownership. I'm aware of museums owned by community colleges that have their own staff run it and pay for it. Here, the individual community members and the Heritage Village Committee took ownership, and what you see here today – every one of these pieces, came with the toil and sweat of community members. The log house is not the only one that was taken apart. The Ehle barn was also taken apart and rebuilt here. The volunteers put it back together so quickly that people didn't realize it was here! It fit so well! The wood was so nicely aged, and it fit so well, it was here for a while before people realized it. Because members of the committee have this sense of ownership, they keep these buildings in repair. They don't wait for them to deteriorate. They repair them, they paint them, they update them, and they have a schedule for all of this. (Burns, 2011)

Burns was grateful for the nature of the relationship with the college. He viewed the Heritage Village Committee as a "gold mine." "All these people with knowledge, energy, and history coupled with such a positive attitude keep it continually getting better. And it's a work in progress, all the time."

Celebrations and Advances

MCC was an active participant in the Michigan Sesquicentennial Heritage Village Celebration from July 27 through August 1, 1987, in the Heritage Village on MCC's Sidney campus. The college had also just celebrated its 20th annual commencement by awarding 200 students with their respective degrees or certificates. And MCC's first LPN class (1967) held its 20-year reunion in the Activities Building. It was a year for celebrations, and in keeping with that focus, Doris Washburn, Green Thumb worker at MCC, planted flowers to form "MCC" on sloping ground by the Activities Building.

Jim Fatka was employed as full-time instructor of language arts, and Jim Peacock's role was changed from part-time to full-time instructor of criminal justice. T. Smith and Denise Edwards were hired to the professional staff. MCC hosted two college instructors from the Peoples' Republic of China for a two-week visit. Professors Yan Bin and Luo Ming learned of MCC's history and culture while sharing much of their own to interested students and community members. Some changes in job titles also became effective, such as the bookstore clerk becoming bookstore supervisor, activities building program manager to recreation program manager, and recorder to registrar. Doser, Chairperson of MCC's Board of Trustees, was elected to the board of directors of the national Association of Community College Trustees.

Faculty also changed. At first, instructors were simply hired to teach and did a good job. But over the years, the college learned how to use faculty participation in overall governance and direction. Faculty members took more and more ownership of the institution. Faculty leadership developed -- not only in bargaining contracts, but in the development of curriculum, and assisting adjunct, non-tenured and tenured faculty to be the best they could be. Veteran instructors developed mechanisms for encouraging, monitoring, overseeing, and assisting to make sure faculty were on track.

Staff became more participative in time, with its members taking more ownership as well, and its own leadership emerging over time. Staff positions became more specialized, and professional development became a key focus.

The year of 1987 was also a time of college expansion in many regards. In Greenville, MCC officially opened a remodeled and newly furnished center for instruction and training, located in the parking lot of the former Jorgesen's West, just off of W. Washington Street. Ground was broken for the new Ionia High School, which would contain classrooms and offices for MCC's instructional program in Ionia. Mort Pomeroy of Pomeroy Management (owner of McDonald's in Greenville and other cities) gave the college $5,000 to develop audio-visual materials to associate with the display of the mastodon bones on MCC's campus, and Lehman donated the display cabinets. And the board asked the state to help fund the expansion of facilities at MCC that would add 19,500 square foot of space. Greiner, Inc. was contracted to update the 1971 master plan.

The calendar year ended with the selection of Dr. Kenneth Snow as vice president of instruction, and Karen Lincoln employed as full-time instructor of nursing. In December, the sixth annual Santa's Super Sunday incorporated the newly established Heritage Village, with hot chocolate and crafts in the Shoen Log House, and tours of the Gaffield School.

During the 1988 spring semester, Montcalm County received a $287,000 grant from the Kellogg Foundation toward the Montcalm Tomorrow project, in which MCC and various staff member were to play a key role.

Interestingly, MCC established a guarantee program for students under which tuition would be refunded for any course not transferable to a senior institution or additional training would be provided free if a vocational student found his or her skill lacking at an entry level.

Another Heritage Village Celebration was held at the village from August 8-12, and a decision was made to make this an annual event. Members would discuss whether five days was too long a period for the celebration. This annual event later became known as Heritage Festival, and would be conducted on the first Thursday, Friday and Saturday of August.

Also by August, the south reading room in MCC's learning resource center was prepared for the arrival of mastodon bones now known as Crystal, and the bones were carefully put into place.

Three additional buildings were donated to Heritage Village: the Sidney Township Hall, a downtown Sidney store building donated by MCC Instructor Christensen and his wife, Missy, and an antique jailhouse from Edmore.

In 1989, MCC Instructor Morford began plans for a student and citizen trip to the People's Republic of China. The trip filled but had to be cancelled at the last minute due to the disorder in China's Tiananmen Square.

The 10th Annual Women's Festival was held on campus. Maureen Burns was the keynote speaker.

Heritage Village received a state grant of $20,000 which was used to renovate and move the old Sidney store and the Sidney Township Hall to Heritage Village.

MCC's Ionia Education Center, built in conjunction with the new Ionia High School, began operations. Several classrooms were utilized, and several courses were slated in general studies. The center anticipated both dual enrolled students from Ionia High School and area non-high-school students as well.

The first series of lectures/concerts sponsored by the Global Awareness Consortium presented several programs under the title of African Awareness. MCC was a member of the Global Awareness Consortium.

Interestingly, as the fall semester began, *The Daily News* slipped a decimal and reported in a headline that MCC had enrolled 19,000 students for the fall semester! The real figure was 1,900.

25th Anniversary

The red letter year of 1990 marked the 25th anniversary of MCC. With a series of events, MCC began an extensive celebration of the initial vote to approve the establishment of the college. As part of the celebration, the college presented a five-part lecture series simply titled Global Awareness, beginning in March, the same month in which the original vote took place. One of the special speakers would be Tatiana Yankelevich, stepdaughter of Nobel Peace Prize winner Andrei Sakharov, sponsored by the Global Awareness Consortium. In June, a 25th anniversary party was held for the public in the Activities Building and outside on a Sunday afternoon. The special event included free refreshments and lively entertainment.

As campus expansion continued, the board authorized spending $100,000 to remodel the Barn Theater. The MCC music department subsequently moved into this remodeled facility, and the bookstore was then moved into its current location.

Failed Millages

In 1991, the board resolved to hold a millage election on October 8, 1991, requesting 1.5 mills. The millage election failed by a vote of 1,349 yes to 1,752 no. On the heels of such forward progress of the college and its growing relationship with the community, this failure was unexpected. However, the millage failure did not deter the school from moving ahead. Just a few months later, the MCC Foundation voted to fund the updating of Heritage Village, the mastodon bones, and the nature trails. The board also authorized the expenditure of $30,000 from Plant Fund monies for expansion of the school's parking facilities. And MCC received word from the Michigan Department of Commerce granting approval of the off-campus nursing program.

With the resignation of Trebian from the Board of Trustees and in appreciation for his contributions to the beautification of the campus and the Trebian Orchard at Heritage Village, he was granted emeritus status. Later, the administrative conference room was named in his honor.

Another attempt at a millage election was held March 2, 1993, but was again defeated. MCC's board held a special meeting to discuss the failed election, and determine how to handle the current financial challenges. After deliberation, the trustees resolved to close the pool for the 1993-94 fiscal year, and hold another election at the time of the annual school election to levy taxes without the reduction required by the state constitution of 1963. However, upon hearing the decision to close the pool, the MCC Foundation expressed its willingness to undertake fund raising designated to allow the opening of the pool.

Despite the many challenges the college was facing, the board also expressed ongoing confidence in President Burns, and commended him for his "excellent leadership" (MCC board minutes). Trustees also authorized a limited opening of the college pool for the following year provided the necessary funds would be raised from outside sources. They also further resolved that the full 1.68 mills allowed after application of the Headlee rollback be levied for operations for 1993-94 and that an additional .08 mill be levied for debt principal and interest payment during the year.

The pool did fully reopen on January 3, 1994, but with changes in prices for most pool programs.

Another election was set for October 8, 1994, to request 1.5 mills for seven years. Several discussions focused on millage election strategies. However, this millage also failed with only a 45-percent level of support from the voters.

In 1995, the MCC board asked the foundation to oversee the renovation of the farmhouse, and presented a tribute to Doser for her 30 years of faithful service on the Board of Trustees.

Fiscal Turning Point

Another millage election date was set for February 14, 1996, with the college asking for an increase of 1.25 mills. Two special meetings were conducted to discuss campaign strategy for the upcoming millage election. This millage passed with 60 percent of the voters casting affirmative ballots.

According to Burns, "This was the fiscal turning point of the institution." He continues, "It changed the college from a struggling institution to a developing one. Up to that time, MCC was doing everything it could to maintain itself. From that point on, however, we had the breathing room necessary to expand, develop, and spread our wings" (Burns, meeting).

Before long, renovations of the farmhouse were completed, and a newly refurbished and newly named Foundation Farmhouse held an open house for the college family and community on October 22. The board resolved that future meetings of the trustees would be conducted in the Foundation Farmhouse.

The college also approved a three-year renewal in 1997 with option for an additional two years of the MCC Greenville Center with Jorgensen Brothers Realty. Carbonelli was named as the new chairperson of the MCC board following Doser's retirement. Janet Shy Campbell was employed as instructional services assistant and would become the director of MCC's bookstore. In November, the college authorized replacing the roof on the Vocational Technical Building (Instruction North) for $44,545.

Lifelong Learners Established

While attending the Michigan Association of Continuing Education and Training annual conference in 1997, Director of Continuing Education Pat Willison learned of the Institute for Learning in Retirement. She loved the concept, and included it in her June 18 management plan for that year, and she also asked Morford to assist. A focus group convened to explore her proposal of "senior citizens and extended learning." Information was gathered in July, a core group assembled in August, and a steering committee organized by September. Initial workshops were offered in October and November of 1997, and the official program rolled out in January 1998 with Morford as the president and Willison as the MCC representative. The organization would take the name, Lifelong Learners. Cliff Bedore served as treasurer.

Doser Building Proposed

Doser and EightCap, Inc. received the 1998 MCC Distinguished Service Award, and agreements were authorized for the construction of the Doser instructional building and related site work at $4,960,239. Bids for the first phase of the campus construction project were actually 12 percent higher than projected. MCC adjusted the budget to $8,257,414 for general operation and $241,000 for the Activities Building. It also reset the in-district tuition at $49.90 per credit hour, out-of-district tuition at $76.55 per credit hour, and out-of-state tuition at $97.70.

In an effort to keep some consistency of campus building nomenclature, the Vocational Technical Building was renamed the Instruction North Building. This also allowed for future use of the building beyond the vocational and technical disciplines, and allowed the move of several of the vocational and technical courses into the soon-to-be opened Beatrice E. Doser Building. On March 10, 1999, the following article appeared in *The Daily News*:

MCC project ahead of schedule

By The Daily News

SIDNEY – Construction of the new vocational-technical building at Montcalm Community College remains ahead of schedule, school officials said.

Jim Lantz, vice president for administrative services, said the work is probably a month ahead of schedule because workers were able to close in the building early.

"It's moving along real well," Lantz said. "Once they have the outside sealed, there is not a lot to slow them down."

Renovation to the upstairs of the Library / Administration Building should be completed this week, he said. Cleaning in the upstairs will take place late this week. Furniture will come in next week.

The administrative office likely will be moved from the downstairs to the upstairs before the end of the month, Lantz said.

Remodeling of the lower level, which will hold the library, will begin after the upper level is complete.

The entire project is scheduled to be completed this summer.

In other business, Lantz said college officials are developing a business plan for a proposed new college facility in Howard City. Existing branch sites are in Greenville, Ionia, and Alma. (*The Daily News*)

Panhandle Area Center

MCC had indeed signed a lease for dedicated space in a soon-to-be constructed community center in Howard City.

The 9,500-square-foot center that was under construction by Cedar West Development, LLC, of Cedar Springs, would include two classrooms and an office that the college would rent. United Memorial Hospital and the Montcalm Alliance also planned to rent spaces in the new building. The new center, located just south of Howard City near the Federal Highway and Lake Montcalm Road intersection, was expected to open in the late fall of 1999.

"We are pleased to see this project come to fruition," stated President Burns. "One of the college's main goals in recent years has been to take programs and services to outlying areas – including the Tri-County Public Schools district. Our long-term lease in this facility is a positive step in increasing our service in the Panhandle area" (T. Smith, MCC news release).

The college planned to offer several fall semester courses at Tri County High School to help launch the initiative. These courses included accounting, child development, social science, English, geometry, and chemistry. Future offerings in the center would be determined by the needs of area residents. Sandra Golden Associates, a research firm, conducted a telephone survey to determine the community's needs and perceptions. Survey results, available in June of that year, helped the college administration determine what courses should be offered.

An official ground-breaking ceremony took place in Howard City on June 16, 1999. Rosemary Horvath reported in *The Daily News*:

> HOWARD CITY - Community leaders turned ground over Wednesday to celebrate building a 10,000-square-foot Montcalm County Community Center here, beginning in July ... Tenants include Montcalm Community College ...
>
> The building site, about 2.5 acres, is located at the village limits in Pierson Township ...
>
> Architect Mark Tomasik of Innovative Design, Grand Rapids, said in addition to providing the space asked for by the tenants, he designed a building that

would be "a magnet for the community. We put together a plan that has a traditional look, with a shingled roof and clock tower in the front …

MCC will have classrooms and office space. (Horvath, June 16, 1999)

At the same time construction was underway in Howard City, several contracts were awarded to successful bidders for items in the new Beatrice E. Doser Building and other areas of renovation, including furniture, signage, and telecommunication wiring. Renovations of the Instruction West Building were also completed, and renovation of the Instruction East Building would be completed before the fall semester began. An authorized lump sum payment of $52,495 was given to the Gratiot-Isabella Regional Education Service District (RESD) for a fiber-optic system for interactive television programming.

Greenville M-TEC Proposed

President Burns also reported that an updated application for a technical education center in Greenville would be submitted in early August. MCC received a state grant and local match that would finance the construction of a $2.5-million Michigan Technical Education Center in Greenville. Horvath again reported:

The 14,675-square-foot-building will be built on land MCC owns, just southwest of Greenville High School. MCC officials are calling the M-TEC a "smart learning" center.

Targeted occupational areas are information technology, manufacturing/production, mechanics and repairers, construction and health occupations. An 11-member board representing area schools, industry, economic development groups, will advise the college board of trustees.

The center will connect with MCC's main campus here and its community learning centers in Ionia, Alma and Howard City. (Horvath, August 1999)

Beatrice E. Doser Building Completed and Dedicated

Of course, the crowning on-campus project of 1999 was the completion of the Beatrice E. Doser Building, named in honor of the Edmore resident who faithfully served on MCC's Board of Trustees for 32 years, and had a significant role in the planning and development of the college.

Doser had just moved to Montcalm County from Los Angeles, Calif., in the early 1960s when the idea of planting a community college first surfaced. She realized she was new to the community, but volunteered to help in any way that she could, even if that meant simply addressing envelopes. She was surprised when she was invited to join the community college planning committee, direct the publicity campaign, and serve as finance chair for the feasibility study. Doser was later elected as a trustee, and then served as chair for many of MCC's formative years. She also served as a member of the MCC Foundation Board of Directors.

An open house was held Sunday, October 10, 1999, to celebrate completion of the $11.4-million campus development project that included its new and renovated facilities. The Beatrice E. Doser Building, along with its enclosed connector to the Activities Building, was dedicated at 2 p.m. Six children from the community, dressed in costumes to represent different vocations, assisted President Burns, Doser, and Board Chairperson Carbonelli in the official ribbon-cutting ceremony. MCC later received a first-place Paragon Award from the National Council for Marketing and Public Relations for the promotion campaign that culminated in the October open house.

The Doser building houses general and computer classrooms, technical equipment, tutoring labs, testing areas, and a skills development center. Its large meeting room, available for community use, has a seating capacity of more than 100. A partition can also create two smaller rooms.

To cap off the campus development project, a new electronic sign was installed on the corner of Sidney Road and College Drive that allowed the computerized display of announcements.

M-TEC Becomes a Reality

By the end of 1999 and approach of 2000, MCC held interviews with firms regarding the M-TEC facility planned for Greenville and employed Duce Simmons Associates as the architect. Several individuals were appointed to the M-TEC Board of Overseers. Estimated costs of the building were $3,300,000.

A ground-breaking ceremony for the M-TEC was conducted June 16, 2000, and progress on the construction of the building quickly ensued. At the same time, MCC authorized The Christman Company to issue subcontract agreements in the amount of $2,220,410 for construction of the M-TEC, now called the Stanley & Blanche Ash Technology & Learning Center.

During the 2001 spring semester, the college learned the construction of the M-TEC was two weeks behind schedule, but was pleased with the completion of the Head Start facilities just south of the water tower and the Instruction North Building in Sidney.

At a board meeting conducted at the new Panhandle Area Community Center in Howard City, the trustees learned that the architect for MCC's Doser building was recognized at the American Institute of Architecture for his work on the structure. They also decided to name the college's nature trails the Kenneth J. Lehman Nature Trails.

During this period of construction, the MCC Foundation responded to three additional recommendations of the college: upgrading the newly named nature trails, supporting child-care in the new Head Start facility on campus, and funding the 2001-02 participation in the Consortium for Community College Development's strategic development and planning project.

Fall 2001 saw the completion of the M-TEC in Greenville, and MCC held a grand opening September 12 at the new facility. A special ribbon-cutting ceremony dedicated the new, 19,000-square-foot M-TEC, followed by guided tours, refreshments, door prizes, and entertainment. The new MCC center was located on four acres at 1325 Yellow Jacket Drive, just south of Greenville High School. It was one of 18 in the state constructed by Michigan community colleges in partnership with the Michigan Economic Development Corporation (MEDC) to provide workplace education and training.

"The M-TEC at Montcalm Community College's Greenville site is the tool that will get and keep employees up to speed," stated Leslie Wood, the newly appointed center coordinator and Director of MCC's Workforce Development Department (T. Smith, MCC news release).

The M-TEC is the place where employers and employees will get what they need – everything from customer service, to computer literacy to plant maintenance training. And with this new center, MCC doesn't require you to sign up for traditional, 16-week, semester-long classes to get where you need to be. Instead, we're offering competency-based instruction through a variety of methods – self-paced, individualized computer software programs; instructor-led coursework; Internet-based and distance learning; or even hands-on applications at your work site – basically, whatever works best" (T. Smith, MCC news release).

The center was funded by MEDC and local donations, and named The Stanley & Blanche Ash Technology & Learning Center in recognition of its foremost donors who supported the center with a $500,000 gift. The MCC Foundation raised $1.3 million in donations from local organizations and individuals including the Bill Braman Family and several other families and businesses. Following a grant request made by MCC and several area businesses, the MEDC promised nearly $2.5 million to help build the center.

"The Ash center actually began more than a year before the MEDC's grant program was introduced," said MCC President Donald Burns. "A few years ago, we began meeting with area business-and-industry leaders to find ways to provide training that would keep their companies solvent and on the cutting edge. We quickly realized the need for a responsive, immediately available local facility to meet these needs." (T. Smith, MCC news release)

An interesting aspect of the training being offered at the M-TEC is that it would be determined by local businesspeople – the same people who employ the workers and who deal with the day-to-day competition in their businesses. The Ash center is to be governed by a board of overseers comprised of business, city and educational leaders. The board reviews training needs and directly links training offered to industry standards. Initial offerings through the center fall into three main categories: workplace skills, technical skills and support services. Workplace skills training covers soft skills like speaking with confidence, responding to change, working in a team, problem solving, and work place ethics. Technical skills training includes information technology (computer literacy), Internet, project tracking, manufacturing and projection (electrical, mechanical, material handling) and business literacy (decision making, understanding customers and the employee's role in the total process).

However, the services at the M-TEC would not solely be for companies and their employees, and employees would not need to wait for their employer to send them for training. "Anyone who believes he or she can benefit from learning additional skills should contact us," Wood said. "One of the beauties of the training available is that it works very well for a single person – or an entire company – trying to improve" (T. Smith).

The center features three seminar rooms, four state-of-the-art computer labs, a study center with attached individual study rooms, and a well-equipped media retrieval room that houses computer programs, CDs and videotapes. The center features an attractive conference and dining room that accommodates up to 100 guests. The conference room and smaller meeting rooms are available for rent to people and organizations.

MCC was also attempting to better serve students in the greater Greenville area by offering credit and non-credit classes in the Ash center. Fourteen credit classes – from cultural anthropology to computer literacy, freshmen English, algebra, and tool & die theory were slated to be offered during the 2001 fall semester. Non-credit courses included classes in computer technology, personal finance, foreign languages, and recreation. The center also would house dual-enrollment courses for high school students. These are college courses for juniors and seniors who met the state's dual-enrollment criteria.

Dignitaries participating in the dedication open house included Michigan's Lt. Gov. Dick Posthumus, Greenville Mayor Jon Aylsworth, and Greenville Area Chamber of Commerce Board President John O'Donald, DDS. ("Briefly," *The Daily News*).

College Growth and Displaced Workers

Calendar year 2002 saw the accomplishments of several MCC Foundation projects, including institutional grants, Heritage Village renovations, MCC's participation in the Strategic Leadership Forum, and the renovation of Barn Theater seating. Thankfully, fall credit headcount enrollment was 7.7 percent higher and credit hour enrollments were 10 percent higher than 2001.

The closing of the Electrolux plant in Greenville was announced in 2003, and MCC began to brace itself and prepare for an influx of displaced workers. As early as January 2004, the college engaged with the Employee Assistance Task Force serving Electrolux workers, and requested $10,000 from the MCC Foundation to assist with activities to serve the displaced workers. Swells in attendance followed.

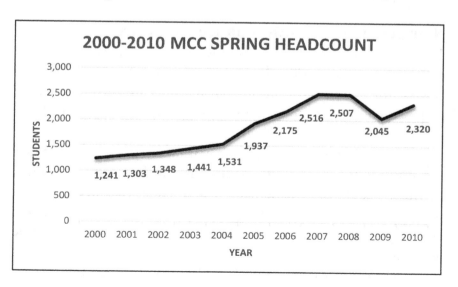

Given MCC's especially important role in the community at the time, Burns personally invited Michigan Governor Jennifer Granholm to deliver the commencement address, and she accepted. Due to the expected large numbers of attendees, the board decided to hold the college's 2004 annual commencement in the Central Montcalm High School gym. As anticipated, the commencement drew the largest audience in MCC's history as Governor Granholm addressed the graduates and their friends and families with words of hope and encouragement. Since that time, every annual commencement has been conducted at the CMHS facility.

There were also shifts in gender percentages now recognized within the student body. During one commencement with more than 100 graduates walking, Burns remembers there were three males that participated. The number of males continued to increase within the student body along with displaced workers. Over time, the student body became older and less traditional (Burns).

MCC's Youth Offender Program (formerly COPE) was carefully reviewed in 2005, with a look at its history, budget, locations, and programming. It later became the Correctional Education Reentry Training program, which was ultimately eliminated when the federal grant expired.

New Science and Maintenance Facilities

Talks also began regarding the need for a new life sciences facility on campus that would provide additional classrooms, botany and chemistry labs, faculty offices, and a full-size nursing lab. Estimated costs for the proposed building and other remodeling projects associated with the new facility came to $7.5 million.

Discussions during the following year included the need for a new maintenance facility, sewage lagoons, and further work at M-TEC. By August 2006, construction and renovation had begun on the new science building, and a bid package for the new maintenance building was ready for distribution and consideration. Expansion of the bookstore was also considered.

A contract was later awarded to Greg Ray Construction for the new maintenance facility in the amount of $265,000, and DSA was named architects for the M-TEC expansion project. The Christman Company was selected as the construction manager for both the M-TEC expansion and the bookstore expansion. The board also voted to name the new life-science facility the Stanley P. Ash Building. By March 2007, MCC approved a construction and completion assurance agreement, a conveyance of property, and a lease and easement agreement for the life science training facility.

On October 19, 2007, MCC unveiled its Stanley P. Ash Building and announced its $2.5-million capital campaign during a ceremony on the Sidney campus. More than 100 guests celebrated the facility, which was named posthumously in honor of the longtime MCC supporter.

MCC Foundation President Thomas Kohn outlined challenges and opportunities that led to the need for enhanced capacity of the college. "Our community needed the ability to train more nurses and workers for industries like United Solar Ovonic in Greenville, and the college needed the resources and facilities to meet these needs," said Kohn (Strautz-Springborn, MCC news release).

Kohn announced the capital campaign to provide a portion of the funding for new and renovated facilities and updated programs. The state capital outlay process awarded MCC $3 million and $3 million was planned from the college's operating budget toward the $8.5-million project.

MCC Director of Institutional Advancement T. Smith said the college raised more than its goal in its *Developing a 21st-Century Community* capital campaign (Strautz-Springborn).

Stanley P. Ash Building and Instruction North Renovations

Ground was broken for the Stanley P. Ash Building in June 2006 and the new building and renovated Instruction East Building, Instruction North Building and Barn Theater were ready for MCC's fall 2007 semester.

The 21,700-square-foot Stanley P. Ash Building is an environment-friendly addition to the college's Sidney campus. The building is Leadership in Energy and Environmental Design (LEED) certified for being environmentally friendly. Features include extensive use of daylight, increased ventilation, outdoor air delivery monitoring, lighting controls, water efficient landscaping, reduced water usage, reduced electrical usage, and recycling of construction water. A kiosk near the entrance displays real-time energy use statistics.

The building includes biology and chemistry laboratories, state-of-the-art nursing classrooms, two lecture auditoriums with seating for 72 and 56, group study areas and faculty offices.

Classrooms were renovated and a ceramics studio, painting studio, photography lab and exhibit space were added to the college's Instruction North Building. Renovations in the Barn Theater, MCC's performing arts facility, provided new, more comfortable seating, wider lighted aisles and a sprinkler system.

"The new Stanley P. Ash Building is crucial as the need for health care workers expands and the level of sophistication in their training increases," said MCC President Burns (Strautz-Springborn). "The art and theater spaces will allow us to provide enhanced opportunities for community enrichment. These facilities will help the college meet our community's educational needs."

The following article appeared in *The Daily News* on October 20, 2007:

New buiding is named for Ash
By Ryan Jeltema
Daily News Staff Writer

SIDNEY – Stanley P. Ash's name appears often when looking back on the beginnings of Montcalm Community College (MCC).

The former owner of Greenville Tool & Die was the college's first Board of Trustees president, the first president of the MCC Foundation, and the first recipient of the Distinguished Service Award.

When the college was struggling to make ends meet only a few years after opening, Ash donated $10,000 so MCC could pay all of its bills on time.

On Friday, MCC officials and community members celebrated completion of a $4.1 million, 21,700-square-foot life science classroom building named in Ash's honor.

"When I think of what he provided here – finances are important – but it was his common sense that was most important," MCC President Donald Burns told an audience of about 100 people. "It is certainly proper and fitting that we are naming this new life sciences building after him."

Ash's widow, Blanche Ash, recalled how he had great hope in helping launch MCC in the mid-1960s that the venture would be successful, that students would and could come to receive a relevant education and that the college would grow and flourish as a pillar in Montcalm County.

"Stan would be pleased with this great building and the improvements that are being made," Blanche Ash said. "I'm sure this is what he hoped for."

Major donor and supporter Bill Braman of Greenville said Stanley Ash's contributions to MCC have enriched lives in Braman's family and the entire community.

"It's no small reason that I feel so good about what is happening here today," Braman said. "This is truly a fine tribute to Stan, who gave so much of himself, and to his wife, Blanche."

... The new building was part of a larger $8.5 million improvement plan for the Sidney and Greenville campuses. The only portion yet to be completed is a $1 million expansion to the Michigan Technical Education Center (M-TEC) in Greenville that is still in the planning stages to house the new Integrated Manufacturing Technology course.

Greenville resident Bill Cook, a longtime supporter and major donor to MCC, said higher numbers of students continue furthering their educations beyond high school year after year like he and other supporters originally intended.

"The greater enrollment has brought a need for more classrooms. But numbers are not the whole story. They are providing a timely education," Cook said, thinking back to when the site selection committee in the 1960s broke ground on the Sidney campus. "Who knew this would all happen here – how this place has grown."

Retired MCC Professor Les Morford said the college has met the pledge that supporters laid out to voters for a millage creating the college.

"MCC has more than lived up to its promise," he said. "When the site selection committee was meeting and trying to get the millage approved, they made the commitment that 'If you approve this, this is what you will get.'" (Jeltema)

No sooner had the dust settled from the new construction and renovation projects, than Burns brought to the board a new five-year master plan and facilities assessment. During a special meeting in February 2008 with the college administrators and Board of Trustees, MCC's leadership discussed and addressed the economic, demographic and development assumptions about Montcalm County and the college, cash flow, and specific projections through 2011. Based on a document distributed by Burns three months earlier, particular aspects of a new strategic plan were also examined as they related to instructional programming, facilities and grounds, technology, student life, and advancement. In a subsequent meeting, the leadership requested $56,000 from the MCC Foundation for landscaping and history projects.

In light of the recent construction of the Ash building and the Ashes' long-term dedication to MCC, the board named Blanche Ash the recipient of the 2008 Distinguished Service Award. The college also renamed the award the Stanley and Blanche Ash Distinguished Service Award. During the 2008 annual commencement, Blanche Ash was awarded an honorary degree.

Burns Retires

In August 2008, Burns announced his intent to retire effective June 30, 2009. The days immediately following his announcement were very quiet days on campus. While everyone supported him in this important decision, there was also a feeling of great loss, for Burns was highly appreciated by fellow administrators, faculty, staff, students, and the community.

By the end of September, MCC contracted the Michigan Leadership Institute to conduct the presidential search process, and by January 2009, four candidates were selected for public interviews: Dr. Patricia Adkins, Robert Ferrentino, J.D., Dr. Anne Monroe, and Dr. William Tammone, the school's vice president for academic affairs.

In March of 2009, Ferrentino was selected to serve as MCC's president by a board vote of 6 to 1.

During one of the last meetings directed by President Burns, MCC's faculty and staff members with an interest in cultural events were assembled in the Trebian Conference Room to discuss the possibility of a coordinated effort on campus to promote the cultural arts. Dean of Arts and Sciences Gary Hauck was appointed as the college's cultural events coordinator. As a result of this appointment, Hauck later founded the Montcalm Area Humanities Council that would also serve as an advisory board to MCC.

A large retirement party was held in Burns' honor in the MCC gym, with hundreds attending. Live music, refreshments, and several speakers celebrated President Burns' long, faithful, and productive tenure at the college.

Reflecting on Burns' accomplishments at MCC, *The Daily News* earlier referred to him as, "A perfect fit" (Horvath, "Burns still enthusiastic").

"I wanted to go overseas. In 1969 Maureen and I left for Madrid."

Accepting the post of director of admissions for the American School of Madrid enabled the couple to experience another culture, an interest they share.

Before he renewed a contract, Burns learned of a job opening at MCC. He applied and took the post. He's never left.

"The concept of a community college hasn't changed in 30 years. The challenge of what a community college should do is huge."

As Burns made the progression from school counselor to college president, he made sure the school reflected the total community. He recruited representatives from local hospitals, the department of corrections, industry and business to build school programs.

Students taking social sciences and humanities are encouraged to incorporate "service learning,' with academic learning. One group [led by Instructor Kenric DeLong] works on an Indian reservation in South Dakota helping with community projects. Another group spent a spring break in Mexico.

It's Burns' opinion that MCC must make an "economic impact on the community and a social impact." One way to achieve that is by broadening the lives and outlooks of students with experiences they would not otherwise have.

Burns is modest about his role in MCC's growth since its meager beginning in 1965. Then there were several hundred students. Now students number several thousand.

"I can't be unbiased about what takes place here. Nor can I take credit for the curriculum that has evolved here. But we do offer broader opportunities than the traditional reading, writing and arithmetic."

Les Morford has a different take.

What's been obvious to him over the years is that "MCC and Don Burns fit. Don is very people-oriented.

He has vision to see what he thinks needs to be done and he gets other people excited about doing it."

When the [prior] school president retired in 1984, the Board of Trustees didn't search for a replacement.

"It was already obvious Don was a man of great integrity. One of the things important to Don is the true use of the word community. The college caters to students in the traditional sense, but there are also students who take two hour courses to help at Greenville Tool & Die (as an example). It's always difficult for a community college to balance all that."

While Burns may not be directly responsible for all the programs, Morford said Burns is "credited for creating an atmosphere for people to create those programs. They know they'll get his support." (Horvath, "Burns still ...)

Though officially retired, Burns continues to be active as president emeritus, and a member of the MCC Foundation. He now serves on the Aquinas College Board of Trustees, and teaches doctoral courses at Ferris State University.

Dr. Donald C. Burns, MCC counselor, dean,
vice president, and fourth president

Crystal the Mastodon was discovered near Crystal in 1986.

Top: The Gaffield Schoolhouse was moved from Amble to MCC in
1986. Bottom: The Shoen Log House was reassembled on campus.

Top: The Shoen Log House before disassembly and reconstruction;
Bottom: The establishment of Heritage Village in 1987

The Ionia Learning Center was constructed in 1989.

Beatrice Doser and Stanley Ash participate in
MCC's 25th anniversary on March 2, 1990.

Top: From left, Dr. Don Burns, MCC Trustee Karen Carbonelli, Congressman Guy Vanderjagt, and MCC Board Chairperson Beatrice Doser in Washington, D.C.; Bottom: MCC's first four presidents, from left, Dr. Donald Fink, Dr. Clifford Bedore, Dr. Herbert Stoutenburg, and Dr. Donald Burns

Top: President Burns waits in anticipation for the results of the 1996 millage election. With him are, left to right, Harold Springsteen, Keith Miller, John Beam, and Jim Fatka. Bottom: The Beatrice E. Doser Building is constructed in 1999.

Top: President Burns celebrates the official opening of MCC's Michigan Technical Education Center in Greenville. Bottom: A group tours the M-TEC while it's under construction.

Michigan Governor Jennifer Granholm spoke
at MCC's 2004 commencement.

Top: From left, President Don Burns, Blanche Ash, and State Representative Judy Emmons break ground for the construction of the Stanley P. Ash Building on MCC's Sidney campus. Bottom: Dr. Burns expresses gratitude to Blanche Ash.

Top: MCC's Stanley P. Ash Building, constructed in 2007, includes science and nursing classrooms and faculty offices. Bottom: The MCC campus after 2007

First tier: Students use the Student Success Center. Second tier: The Beatrice E. Doser Building lobby displays globally-themed artworks created by MCC staff and students. Third tier: Native American Dioramas in the Doser building; Fourth tier: From left, indoor sculpture by staff member Kyle Shattuck, replica of *Nike of Samothrace*, and outdoor sculpture by Dr. James Brown, MCC instructor

Chapter 5

---◆·◆·◆---

Student Success, Global Awareness, and Cultural Enrichment

MCC's Fifth President

In July 2009, MCC welcomed Robert C. Ferrentino, JD, as its fifth president. Prior to coming to MCC, Ferrentino spent more than 25 years in community college education. He served as an adjunct instructor and program director of marketing services at Lansing Community College, and vice president of academic affairs at Muskegon Community College. Prior to his roles in education, he practiced law and was employed at the Ford Motor Co.

Ferrentino earned a bachelor's degree in marketing and a master's degree in business administration from Northern Illinois University, and a doctor of jurisprudence degree from the Thomas M. Cooley Law School.

"I have always heard great things about MCC from my colleagues," Ferrentino said. "MCC is a great place and it feels like a natural fit. I can't wait to be part of the community. I am looking forward to meeting people and to becoming involved in the community" (*Sentinel Standard*).

Board Chairperson Karen Carbonelli said, "One of our primary concerns was to find the right person who will reach out into the community. We believe that Bob is very community minded and that his past experience is going to be a real benefit to MCC" (*Sentinel Standard*). In his prior roles, Ferrentino was active in Rotary Club, area school districts, sports programs, and the Michigan Occupational Deans Administrative Council.

Ryan Jeltema, Assistant News Editor, wrote of Ferrentino's first week for *The Daily News*:

> SIDNEY – Bob Ferrentino probably hasn't met as many people in a week as he just did in his first full week as Montcalm Community College's fifth president.
>
> After officially taking over for President Emeritus Donald Burns on July 1, Ferrentino said he spent much of his first week meeting staff, students, and community members while getting a lay of the land.
>
> "I'm getting accustomed to being here," he said. "I've been meeting a lot of people and wandering around campus. I'm starting to get in the swing of my regular meetings and stuff."
>
> Ferrentino, 54, said MCC and the community are welcoming him with open arms. "I'm pleasantly surprised with how easily I've been accepted," he said. "I'm pleased that that has been the case. So far it just feels right – it feels natural."
>
> ... Montcalm Community College (MCC) Board of Trustees President Karen Carbonelli believes Ferrentino's broad background of experience will serve him well as president.
>
> "He's a good communicator and a people person," she said. "I think his law degree will serve us well. It teaches how to find answers and negotiate."
>
> Ferrentino said the decision to leave Muskegon was tough.
>
> "It was a hard couple days packing up my things and saying goodbyes," he said. "But I knew I was doing what I want. If I was going to fulfill my goal, now was the time to do it."

Theresa Sturrus, who worked closely with Ferrentino for more than four years and has taken over his duties on an interim basis in Muskegon, said he has all the tools to effectively lead MCC into the future.

"Bob has always been a strong community supporter. He has been involved a lot in the community he lived in," she said. "That's always a positive for any college. He likes to build people up. He's just a real positive person. He's going to be a great leader."

Ferrentino plans to spend his first few months at MCC getting acclimated to the institution and its culture.

When that initial period of "learning who's who and what's what" is complete, Ferrentino plans to dive into working on a long-term strategic plan for MCC.

"This place is running great but there are always ways to look at things differently," he said. "We'd all agree that we need to take the next step of our vision of where the college is and where it's headed."

Ferrentino sees dwindling revenues and resources as the biggest challenges he'll have to face over the next couple years.

"Certainly there are a lot of issues with dollars and cents," he said. "Our resources are diminishing. We have to be smart about what we're doing. That means we need to look at alternative sources of funding. We've already discussed our ideas of what's important." (Getting Situated - New MCC president completes his first full week on the job meeting staff, students, community members)

A presidential inauguration ceremony and reception was held November 6, 2009.

One of Ferrentino's first priorities was to revisit and revise the college's mission, vision and values, and then to develop MCC's new strategic plan.

For this purpose, he convened a variety of meetings and focus groups throughout the college family and community. Ferrentino explained:

> These are exciting times, times of both challenge and opportunity that demand the best we have to give. This strategic plan serves as our roadmap to meeting the future head on as it reaffirms our vision, mission and values. A benchmark for future program development at Montcalm Community College, the plan is a result of the collaborative efforts of numerous groups of college stakeholders. Many planning meetings were held both on and off campus, engaging many of our colleagues, students, and community members in spirited discussions designed to bring out our best. This inclusive process and open dialogue have resulted in a plan containing a robust blend of strategies sure to move the institution, and our community, forward.
>
> We are thankful for the continued support of the people we serve and we remain committed to our mission of serving a community of learners. (Ferrentino)

That collaboration resulted in the following.

Vision

Montcalm Community College is west-central Michigan's preeminent provider of and preferred choice for education, training, and lifelong learning opportunities.

Mission

MCC is a leader in creating a learning community, contributing to shared economic, cultural, and social prosperity for all our citizens.

Values

Montcalm Community College subscribes to the following institutional values:

We provide a caring environment for our students, staff, and community. We expect competence and the pursuit of excellence from our students and staff. We work in concert with our stakeholder communities to advance the philosophy of lifelong learning. We are committed to providing open access and fostering success for all of our learners. (Strategic Plan)

Strategies and Goals

In efforts to improve communication with internal and external stakeholders, some strategies were chosen to develop a comprehensive marketing plan, implement an integrated communication plan aimed at students, alumni, and community members, and enhance outreach efforts to universities and other colleges, community partners, and other MCC supporters.

Plans included the use of technology to improve internal communication of relevant information, and a goal to maintain and improve existing quality communication efforts targeted to all college stakeholders.

With a view to maintaining and enhancing MCC's sound financial condition and fiscal integrity, strategies were also identified to seek diversified funding opportunities to supplement general fund capabilities, develop and implement improved advancement efforts targeted at donors, prospective donors, and alumni, improve operational efficiencies to help control costs and reduce waste, and use technology as appropriate to streamline processes and creatively incorporate available resources. Other objectives called for development of a plan to enhance revenues from academic programming, and improvement of effective budget planning and monitoring to ensure continuation of a sound financial condition.

MCC reaffirmed its commitment to provide professional development opportunities for all employees, explore creative approaches to improving academic programs and schedules, develop innovative approaches to increase student success through the Achieving the Dream initiative, and create plans to secure alternative funding to support purchases of needed equipment and the offering of special programming.

The college also pledged its commitment to foster a culture of entrepreneurship where employee empowerment and creative problem-solving are the norms, and celebrate successes.

To continue MCC's commitment to continuous quality improvement, new strategies were also identified to use and support quality improvement systems to enhance campus operations, maintain Academic Quality Improvement Program (AQIP) standards of accreditation, increase academic excellence by improving classroom programming, and use resources available through Achieving the Dream, AQIP, Continuous Quality Improvement Network, and Michigan College Access Network initiatives to support and improve campus operations.

It was determined to establish a culture of data-informed decision making, continue to pursue methods to improve the delivery of student services while maintaining present standards of quality service, and foster a culture of continuous quality improvement so that all colleagues understand the importance of, and the need for, this effort.

In addition, the college resolved to consistently seek out partnerships that promise to improve the effective and efficient use of resources by expanding MCC's academic programs in partnership with other institutions of higher education, and explore options and create a plan for better use of, and improved programming at, off-campus facilities, enhance campus operating efficiencies through partnerships and collaborations with suppliers and other educational entities.

Finally, leadership resolved to maintain and further cultivate relationships with K-12 districts, intermediate school districts, and parents in MCC's district and service area, solidify and expand relationships with local, state, and national organizations relevant to the college's mission, expand MCC's partnerships with business and industry, and continue to consistently deliver the message that MCC is the community's partner in lifelong learning.

Student Success

One of the major shared concerns of President Ferrentino and the other administrators was the need for improved student success. For this reason, student success became the institutional focus for concerted quality improvement, and the decision to join forces with Achieving the Dream, a national reform network dedicated to community college student success and completion, focused primarily on helping low-income students and students of color complete their education and obtain market-valued credentials.

On April 14, 2010, the board approved a resolution to request funds from the MCC Foundation Board of Directors to support the college's participation in the Achieving the Dream grant program, and MCC became a recipient of an Achieving the Dream: Community Colleges Count grant, effective on July 1, 2010. A readiness assessment was completed and a data report was generated to determine strategies to address five main student cohort outcomes:

1. Successfully complete developmental instruction course requirements within two years.
2. Successfully complete the initial college-level or gateway courses within three years.
3. Successfully complete the courses they take with a grade of C or better.
4. Persistence and Retention:
   a. Persistence term to term.
   b. Retention from year to year.
5. Attain a certificate or degree (credential) within four years.

Campus-wide kickoff activities occurred in 2010, and 2011 was the first year of implementation. The college continued participation through the summer of 2014. Key benefits of this relationship included technical assistance and professional development that impacted faculty, staff, and support staff throughout the institution.

To address these outcomes, four strategies or "interventions" were identified. All four ran during the full timeframe of MCC's Achieving the Dream involvement and are still operational. The first strategy was to redesign the school's method of delivering developmental education for those students not ready for college math or English.

Developmental education courses in reading, writing, and math have traditionally been designated and run outside of the English and math college-level course departments. However, a decision was made to move developmental coursework from a DVED (developmental) designation directly into the respective academic departments (English or math), so that developmental work feeds seamlessly into the intended academic area. English Instructor Jamie Hopkins and Math Instructor Brianne Lodholtz were hired specifically to strengthen the college's developmental education program. The instructors work together by subject area to be sure that a common progression occurs. Coursework is now delivered within a classroom instead of an open lab.

The admissions policy changed so that beginning in fall 2011, students who tested below 7th grade competency levels in writing, reading, or math would be referred to local literacy councils. This partnership with the literacy councils allows students to get the one-on-one tutoring they need before coming to MCC. "Since implementing the changes in fall semester of academic year 2012, successful developmental course completion (grade of C or better) has increased 11 percentage points (about a 20% increase)" (Lund, 2014).

A student success center was also created, and Jessica Gilbertson was hired as the coordinator/director to oversee and monitor supplemental instructional areas related to developmental coursework. A corps of student mentors provide in-class supplemental instruction in some developmental reading, math, and English courses, and other classes as necessary. Staff development is provided to the mentors/supplemental instruction leaders. "Over the past three years, data has shown that students who participate in the voluntary supplemental instruction sessions have higher course success rates than students who may be in the same supplemental instruction course section but do not attend the voluntary sessions" (Lund, 2014).

As a result of the reformation of the purpose of the former testing center in 2011, MCC's student success center expanded the college's services by creating a full-service center geared toward curriculum support for students in the Beatrice E. Doser Building on the college's Sidney campus. In addition, certain support services have also been expanded to the Greenville campus. The position of student success director was established to supervise the center's staff and activities. In 2015, student success center services included:

- Academic skills assessment (COMPASS) to help students determine their readiness for college-level courses
- Academic counseling; Services for students needing accommodations including note-takers, interpreters and books on tape
- Free tutoring, from both professionals and peers
- HelpMe, an online and drop-in student success tutor
- Supplemental instruction
- Credit courses in college reading, writing, basic math, and study skills
- A testing center where instructors can send students to take proctored make-up and online exams
- Proctored testing for Michigan Virtual Learning Community students
- Work-Keys® - job skills assessment for those seeking National Career Readiness Certification.

Other Advances

In efforts to serve the MCC family more effectively and achieve better financial stewardship, the college changed its food service to a Subway restaurant, and its campus bookstore to a Barnes & Noble. Subway opened in the northwest corner of the Activities Building on August 1, 2010, and Barnes & Noble opened December 12, 2011.

Headlee Override Elections

The college did, however, experience some setbacks. Early in 2011, a proposal was made to restore the present and future millage reduced by Headlee for community college operating purposes:

Shall the currently authorized charter millage rate limitation on the amount of taxes which may be assessed against all property in Montcalm Community College,

Michigan, for operating purposes be increased by not more than .2708 mill ($0.2708 on each $1,000.000 of taxable valuation) to be used for all purposes authorized by law; if approved, the estimate of revenue the community college will collect the first year of levy, 2011, approximately $587,138? (MCC board minutes, January 12, 2011)

Despite concerted efforts to educate the public on the importance of this measure, the special public election failed to pass on August 2, 2011. In fact, there were two Headlee Override elections that year, and both failed. However, the college family rallied in a series of cost-reduction decisions, and campus life continued to flourish.

By April of 2012, the board approved a resolution estimating MCC's 2012-2013 fiscal-year revenues at 2.72 mills from property taxes and $3,050,000 from state appropriations. It set MCC's in-district tuition at $87 per credit hour, out-of-district tuition at $164 per credit hour, out-of-state tuition at $244 per credit hour, correspondence tuition at $223 per credit hour and the college service fee at $14 per contact hour effective with the fall 2012 semester.

Bill Braman Family Center for Education

April 2013 saw the addition of MCC's newest facility, the Bill Braman Family Center for Education on the college's Greenville campus. Ground was broken one year earlier on the site of the former Montcalm County 4-H Fairgrounds, purchased by the college in 2010, and next to the Stanley & Blanche Ash Technology & Learning Center (formerly M-TEC, now the Ash TLC). The new building, named after the former MCC trustee and pioneering fruit farmer, features technology labs for advanced manufacturing, increased health-related training options, renewable energy studies, flexible classroom configuration for access to university-level programming, and additional space for noncredit lifelong learning and dual-enrollment classes. Funds for the $5.4-million facility were raised during a capital campaign titled *Creating Futures Strengthening Partnerships* that engaged members of the community and MCC family, with Braman as a lead donor.

During an official dedication and ribbon-cutting ceremony, Braman said, "Our future and prosperity as a community depends on our ability to increase the educational level of the present and future workforce to meet the demands of today's economy." He added, "This new facility became a reality through partnerships and conglomerations. It's a result of many individuals and organizations working toward a common goal to create a brighter future" (Cory Smith, 2013). More than 100 guests attended the ceremony, and heard remarks from Braman, Board Chairperson Carbonelli, MCC Foundation President Tom Kohn, Representative Rick Outman, Senator Judy Emmons, and President Ferrentino.

"Advances in technology, health care, manufacturing, business, communication, and many other aspects of our society," said Ferrentino, "call for a better educated workforce." Ferrentino gave the charge for a fresh emphasis on workforce development (T. Smith, 2013).

One Book One County Montcalm Merges with MCC

In 2005, Maureen Burns launched a county-wide reading program as part of the national One Book One County movement. She coordinated with local libraries and book clubs, and featured both discussion groups and special programs. In 2009, a mutual interest resulted in an official partnership between One Book One County Montcalm and MCC. A planning committee emerged with members Maureen Burns, Shelly Springborn, Jody Butler, and Gary Hauck. Later members included Carole Cole, Laura Powers, Daniel Peterson, Kelsie Stoltenow, Karen Maxfield, Kelsey Shattuck and Samantha Mack. Book-selection committees were also formed each year beginning 2010 to 2014. Book purchases were arranged through the college bookstore, kick-off unveilings occurred each May in the Ash TLC, and closing programs were normally conducted in the performing arts center at Greenville High School.

As MCC launched its 50th anniversary year in fall 2014, One Book One County celebrated its 10th year anniversary with additional programs and an anniversary celebration on the Greenville campus. The 10 selections from 2005 to 2014 were: *Kite Runner* – Khaled Hosseini,

My Sister's Keeper - Jodi Picoult, *Water for Elephants* – Sara Gruen, *Lay that Trumpet in our Hands* – Susan Carol McCarthy, *They Poured Fire on Us from the Sky* – Benson Deng, Alephonsion Deng, Benjamin Ajak, and with Judy A. Bernstein, *Friday Night Lights* – H.G. Bissinger, *Look Me in the Eye* – John Elder Robison, *Major Pettigrew's Last Stand* – Helen Simonson, *The Language of Flowers* – Vanessa Diffenbaugh, and *Me Before You* – Jojo Moyes.

"After 10 years, it's bigger than ever," M. Burns said. "Our goal is to come together as a county, to grow, learn and discuss; the related programs fill that purpose" (Daily News, May 16, 2014). Cole also noted the important role played by the program's sponsors including Chemical Bank, Stafford Media, MCC and the MCC Foundation.

MCC Reads

While One Book One County Montcalm focused on the community during the summer months and early fall, MCC Reads was established to create a community of readers at MCC during the academic year. The initial MCC Reads Committee was comprised of English Instructor Hopkins, MCC Library Director Katie Arwood and MCC Dean of Instruction Hauck. The group selected a title and coordinated events in support of the title's message and theme. The group's goal was to use the reading experience of a common text to encourage reading in new and reluctant readers, inspire long-time readers, create reading habits that benefit the reader and offer a common subject for reflective discussion, community-wide.

The first season of MCC Reads was January 13 to March 25, 2014. The inaugural book was *The Art of Racing in the Rain* by Garth Stein, a heart-wrenching but deeply funny and ultimately uplifting story of family, love, loyalty and hope. This was a beautifully crafted and captivating book about the wonders and absurdities of human life ... as only a dog could tell it. Movie and craft events, discussions, and a pet food and supply drive to benefit the Montcalm County Animal Shelter were held. The book was used in an MCC English class, with the 12th-grade English students at Central Montcalm High School and elsewhere on campus and in the community.

Campus Art

In an effort to enhance the cultural climate and learning environment on MCC's Sidney and Greenville campuses, a significant series of art acquisitions and installations were made possible from 2009 through 2014, thanks in large part to the MCC Foundation and Community College Enrichment Fund bequeathed by Stanley and Blanche Ash.

Sidney campus acquisitions included four large Native American Dioramas purchased from the Cranbrook Institute, photographs of the Montcalm Amish community taken by Grand Rapids Press photographer Lance Wynn, a set of Italian photographs by Dan Watts donated by the Ronald McDonald House of West Michigan, a statue of the *Winged Nike of Samothrace* given by the Port Huron Historical Museum, Grand Rapids ArtPrize pieces (canvas art and outdoor sculpture) created by MCC Instructor Dr. James Brown, MCC Create art competition works by students and staff, and international artifacts and photographs taken by Hauck, who also coordinated the art acquisitions.

MCC Create was a campus-wide art competition in 2011 that invited works of various media to be submitted and displayed throughout the campus. Cash awards were given and entries needed to epitomize a global theme. Finalists were: Debbie Bell (adjunct instructor), Susan Moss (staff member), Katrina Soper (student), and Susanna Yoder (alumnus). Their works are on permanent display in the Beatrice E. Doser Building lobby under the caption Think Globally. That main entrance to the international hall also includes Art Instructor Carolyn Johnson's European photo collection, taken during MCC's study abroad programs.

For the Greenville campus, an art show by the Montcalm Area Art Association was held in the Bill Braman Family Center for Education during October 2013, and a work by MAAA member and MCC Administrative Assistant Moss featuring Greenville's main street was selected to be on permanent display in the TLC. Coleen J. Venema of the Montcalm County 4H Fair donated pictures of the last fair at the fairgrounds before it was purchased by MCC as the site for the Braman center. A large aerial picture of the fairgrounds is now permanently exhibited in the foyer of the center, along with photographic works of the heritage of industry selected by Vice President for Student and Academic Affairs Rob Spohr.

Student Enrichment

MCC's student development department has grown to include a variety of clubs, organizations, and personal enrichment opportunities. Those clubs and organizations include the following.

Alpha Tau Alpha is MCC's Chapter of the Phi Theta Kappa Honor Society for Two-Year Colleges. To qualify for membership, students must complete a minimum of 12 MCC credit hours with a minimum of 3.5 GPA.

The Art Club offers extracurricular opportunities to explore the artistic world.

The Bass Club extends opportunities for members who like to fish.

Business Professional of America is the leading career technical student organization for students pursuing careers in business management, office administration, information technology and other related career field. Students may compete in BPA events against other college students at both the state and national levels.

The Culture and Travel Club promotes domestic and international travel among students by providing information, support, opportunities and reflection.

The Drama Club provides experience in all areas of theater including acting, directing, and stage crew.

The Electronics Club teaches problem-solving techniques of industrial electronics and radio fundamentals through amateur radio.

The Equality Club brings together students to support one another, provide a safe place to socialize and create a platform for activism to fight inequality.

The GHOST Hunters Of Sidney Township scientifically and critically investigates the paranormal.

The Golf Club offers golfing for fun and learning.

The Justice Studies Club furthers learning and socializing for the benefit of understanding.

The Losers Club promotes weight loss and physical fitness in a supportive and fun environment.

The Math Honor Society and Club makes math fun.

The Music Club gathers students who share an interest in music.

The Religion and Philosophy Club explores religion and philosophy.

The Native American Club explores the culture and history of Native Americans.

The Rotoract Club provides opportunities for young men and women to enhance the knowledge and skills that will assist them in personal development, to address the physical and social needs of their communities, and to promote better relations between all people worldwide through Rotary International's framework of friendship and service.

The Volleyball Club spreads awareness of volleyball as a sport and improves personal skills.

The Veterans Club assists student veterans and their dependents in reaching their goals in life.

MCC encourages the development and growth of new clubs and organizations. Each club is led by student officers and is advised by an employee. A campus-wide club day is conducted each semester for information, recruitment, and communication.

Study Abroad

From 2009 through 2015, MCC endeavored to establish a consistent set of opportunities for its students and instructors to study abroad. These included trips to France, Costa Rica, Great Britain, Mexico, Italy and China.

In 2009, MCC took students to Mexico, led by Dr. Maria Suchowski. The college added four courses to its curriculum that focus on the different aspects of studying abroad; the study abroad course is offered as a humanities, social science, environmental sciences or business course, so students can choose which discipline they want to use as a primary lens when studying abroad.

Performing Arts Coordinator Val Vander Mark led a trip to London, Bath and Stonehenge in 2010, and in 2011, she accompanied Visual Arts Coordinator Johnson on a trip she led to Rome, Pompeii, Florence and Paris.

"Both times we took students who had never been overseas, and in some cases had never been on a plane. It was a life-changing experience for them to see things they had only seen in books – like famous places and art," Vander Mark said (Mack, 2014).

Johnson remembers one particular student from the Rome trip well because of how the trip helped her grow:

> "During that trip, I had a student who was pretty inexperienced with travel," Johnson said. "This student had never been outside of Michigan but dreamt of going to Rome. I did a lot of one-on-one advising before the trip, but with all of the pre-trip planning, including getting a passport, this student started to enthusiastically solve her own problems, including getting a second job to pay for the trip. By the time we were travelling, she became very independent and absorbed every detail of the historic and cultural experiences like a sponge" (Mack).

Cultural Events

President Ferrentino continued to support and encourage the advancement of cultural events on campus. "I'm crucially interested in advancing cultural enhancement on campus, because I have also learned so much outside of the classroom – in the world of cultural events. To me, being a well-rounded individual is an absolute essential" (Ferrentino, 2014 interview).

Since fall 2009, a coordinated cultural events calendar has been provided for the campus family with an array of lectures, art shows, musical programs, and special events. Some of these had been established, and some were new. Highlights included an art show by Charlene Jeter of Detroit; an African art display on loan from Kendall College of Art; two performance/lectures by Maestro David Lockington, conductor of the Grand Rapids Symphony; a sculpture presentation by Dr. Joseph Becherer, Curator of the Frederick Meijer Gardens and Sculpture Park; prisoner art shows; a presentation by Winona Duke; a concert performed by Grammy Award winner Bill Miller; a concert by Michael Locke and the Repeat Offenders; a presentation by author Brian Stout on preserving Michigan's trees; and a concert performance by recording artist Max Colley III and his jazz band.

From 2009 to 2014, an annual international symposium was conducted, with speakers from Turkey, Indonesia, Eretria (Africa), Nigeria, Kenya, Greece, Romania, Pakistan, India, Japan, China, and Bosnia. The purpose of the symposium was to bring a new understanding of global perspectives. The Philosophy and Religion Club also invited a Buddhist monk, Muslim imam, Roman Catholic priest, and an evangelical Christian to participate in a symposium on religious beliefs. Another was conducted with a theist, an atheist, and an agnostic, to address the issue of faith and inquiry.

An annual Veterans Day ceremony is held on campus every November 11 at 11 am. MCC veterans are recognized and a moment of silence is observed for those who offered the ultimate sacrifice.

Annual jazz day presentations were facilitated by Language Arts Instructor Fatka, and Social Science Instructor DeLong gave yearly Constitution Day lectures for students and the community. Johnson's drama class presents a fall and spring play, and the MCC music department has continued to present both a fall and spring concert. With 2013 came the addition of the MCC philharmonic orchestra with Charlotte Lothian serving as its first director.

Ash Lectureship

MCC's Stanley and Blanche Ash Lectureship series was established in 2013 to increase the community's awareness of key issues of global and domestic importance with nationally and internationally known speakers and authors. The first three featured speakers were Cleo Paskal, Dr. Annie Dandavati, and Dr. Amy Richards.

Paskal, international speaker and author, presented a lecture to more than 100 students, staff and community members on climate change, geo-politics, and energy independence February 11, 2014 on MCC's Sidney campus. Paskal is the author of the book *Global Warring*.

Dandavati, chair and professor of political science and director of international studies at Hope College, presented Land of the Pharoahs: Three Years after the Arab Awakening April 10 on MCC's Greenville campus. Dandavati told of her experiences as an eye witness to the Egyptian Revolution of 2011 while serving as a visiting professor at the American University in Cairo.

Richards, author, speaker and consultant with the World Affairs Council, presented Global Responsibility in the Digital Age October 8 on MCC's Greenville campus and MCC's Sidney campus.

Moving Into the Future

Entering its 50th anniversary year, MCC made a series of significant strides, moving into the future. A concerted marketing plan was put into effect, with billboards, open house college days, full use of media, and targeted recruitment. New partnerships in workforce development were established, and robotic technology was introduced at the Greenville campus. An Early College was established on campus, for high school students to engage in full collegiate curriculum during their secondary education, and be able to graduate with both a high school diploma and associate degree after "13th grade." Shannon Tripp was appointed as director, and Melissa Ausua, Dean Gage, and Patricia Yonker were hired as full-time Early College instructors.

A series of reports from the MCC Foundation tracked its growth through the days of 33 former directors (including 8 active emeritus) to the present time with 17 current directors, plotting steady fund growth since the first treasurer's report in 1982.

1982 - $3,621
1992 - $414,252
2002 - $2.3 million
2012 - $8.6 million
2015 - $14 million

Over the years, the foundation has supported scholarships, grants, and building projects. It has helped to make possible an autoclave, the mastodon exhibit, the 25th anniversary celebration, the nature trails, the M-TEC, Achieving the Dream, Early College, and this history project.

Millage Renewal

Calendar year 2014 ended on a high note, with the public vote on November 4 to renew MCC's millage. This came just two days after the combined concert of the MCC Alumni and Friends Choir and 55-piece Philharmonic Orchestra performing the concert, Music of the Seas. The Music of the Seas served as a powerful allegory of the waves, tides, and successful journeys in quest of the distant shore.

Robert C. Ferrentino, JD, MCC's fifth president

Top: Maureen Burns greets the audience at One Book One County Montcalm's 10th annual closing program at the Greenville High School performing arts center. Middle: Gary Hauck joins Maureen Burns in greeting guests for a One Book panel discussion. Bottom: Hauck welcomes guests to the One Book 10th Anniversary kickoff.

Arial view of Montcalm Heritage Village, August 2, 2014

Top tier: Heritage Festival at Montcalm Heritage Village; Second tier: Jean Brundage chaired the Heritage Village Committee and docents worked the Blacksmith Shop. Third tier: Views of Heritage Festival; Fourth tier: MCC alumnus Jared Hauck wedded Rachel Spring-Frank at Heritage Village in 2014.

MCC's study abroad groups to Paris, London and Pompeii, led by Instructors Carolyn Johnson and Val Vander Mark in 2010 and 2011

Top: Bill Braman and the Bill Braman Family Center for Education constructed in 2012 on MCC's Greenville campus; Bottom: An aerial view of the Montcalm County Fairgrounds before becoming part of MCC's Greenville campus

Top: International art decorates the hallway in the Doser Building. Bottom: Adjunct instructors gather for the 2014-2015 adjunct academy.

Some of MCC's outstanding alumni

Chapter 6

Alumni –
by Shelly Strautz-Springborn

Brian Calley was sworn in as America's youngest Lieutenant Governor in January 2011. He was just 34. An Ionia native, he spent a decade working as a community banker before Michigan voters elected him as a state representative in 2007. He continued to serve two terms in the House of Representatives prior to being elected with Governor Rick Snyder in 2010.

Calley attended Montcalm Community College in 1995 and 1996, while he was still a student at Ionia High School. Through a partnership between the college and area high schools, dual enrolled students are simultaneously enrolled in high school and in one or more college classes. The classes are taken for both college and high school credit.

"I was fortunate that my high school had a dual enrollment program set up with MCC," Calley says. "My guidance counselor explained how taking MCC general education courses would be a great start for my college education. I am very glad I listened. It was a great head start on my degree."

Calley earned a bachelor's degree in business administration from Michigan State University in 1998 and a Master of Business Administration Degree from Grand Valley State University in 2000. He says his experience at MCC helped him make a smooth transition from high school to college.

"I often hear people reminisce about how intimidating their first college experience was. That wasn't me," Calley says. "MCC provided a caring learning environment that helped me set goals and pushed me to achieve them. It was a comfortable transition into higher education."

Calley has often been recognized by his colleagues as a bold leader with a commitment to reaching across the aisle to bring together political parties. He has been named one of the "Ten Outstanding Young Americans" by the United States Junior Chamber and one of Crain's Detroit Business's "40 under 40." Other honors include the Small Business Association of Michigan's "Legislator of the Year" and Portland's "Outstanding Citizen of the Year."

"I learned at MCC the value of lifelong learning from people who genuinely cared about my future," he says. "Looking back, I feel fortunate that my first college experience was at a place like MCC."

As the parent of a child with autism, Calley is active in statewide autism advocacy. "I understand the tremendous challenges families face and want to help others in any way I can," he says.

In his spare time, Calley can be found cheering on the MSU Spartans, playing the piano or even playing keyboard in a band from time to time. "Montcalm Community College cares about your success – they truly cared about mine," he adds. "MCC is a place where the instructors come with real world experience in the subjects they teach, and they show you how to thrive in our complex economy. And at the end of the day, they still know their students by name.

"MCC made a positive impact in my own life and in the lives of countless people I meet across Michigan," he adds. "It's an important part of our higher education system so make the most of what they have to offer."

Calley and his wife, Julie, live in Portland, Michigan, with their three young children.

(This cameo was originally published in 2013.)

Steve Foster is the Greenville Tool & Die Human Resources Director who credits Montcalm Community College for providing the solid educational foundation that started him down his career path more than 40 years ago.

A 1966 graduate of Greenville High School, Foster began his studies at MCC in 1967. In 1968, he was the first student to earn an associate degree in arts and sciences from the fledgling college. A strong commitment to education has been part of his life ever since.

"I think back to my time at MCC as the most enjoyable of my college years," Foster says. "I enjoyed the small town atmosphere. I knew everyone, including the instructors and Dr. Don Fink, the college president."

Foster credits MCC's faculty and staff for helping him choose a career path and for preparing him to continue his education at Michigan State University (MSU), where he earned a bachelor's degree in business administration in 1970.

"MCC prepared me well for the next level," Foster says. "My courses transferred and I hit the ground running at MSU."

Steve Foster began his career as a management trainee with LexaLite Corporation in Charlevoix, a producer of plastic injection molds for the lighting industry. After relocating to the Greenville area with his family, he went to work at the former Process Equipment Corporation in Belding. There for 10 years, he eventually became the company's sales manager. Foster has served as GTD's Human Resources Director since 1982, when he was hired by company founder Stanley P. Ash. In his position, Foster is responsible for personnel, coordinating the company's apprenticeship programs and employee training, public relations, internal communications, and assisting with a variety of other marketing and sales efforts including printed materials and the company's Web site. Foster says until Ash's death in 2004, he was more than a company owner and supervisor – he was a mentor and a friend.

"From the beginning, he pushed and encouraged me to become more involved in our communities, particularly with our educational institutions," Foster says. "A staunch believer in education and training, Stan echoed a number of times the importance of partnering with these institutions."

Throughout the years, Foster has volunteered with a number of committees and local organizations including the Education Foundation of Greenville, the Montcalm Area Intermediate School District Board of

Education, MCC's Michigan Technical Education Center (M-TEC) Board of Overseers, the American Apprenticeship Round Table, the American Cancer Society's Montcalm County Relay for Life, the annual Montcalm Challenge Food Drive, advisory boards with the Montcalm Area Career Center and MCC, and several other groups. He believes that volunteering enhances individuals as well as the organizations they are affiliated with.

"It is quite common in this day and age to have a job description that is broad in scope, with employees wearing a number of different hats at the same time," Foster says. "It's also important to be connected in our communities – to always keep learning." Foster's commitment to education shines.

"Through the years, I have strongly encouraged high school graduates to attend MCC," he says, "particularly those who have not yet identified a career path.

"The experts tell us that knowledge and technology now doubles about every 14 months. They also tell us that today's graduates can expect a number of career and job changes during their lifetime. Theoretically, if you are not spending at least some time each day learning new things, you are getting behind," Foster says. "Learning is not just for your well-being and fulfillment – it is required for your very livelihood." [Foster received MCC's Stanley and Blanche Ash Distinguished Service Award in 2010.]

(This cameo was originally published in 2011.)

Gary Frisbie is living his childhood dream. As a commercial pilot with Expressjet Airlines, based out of Chicago, Ill., Frisbie has more than 30 years of experience in the cockpit.

"I was in love with airplanes since I can remember. As I grew up, I wanted to be a pilot," he says. "But not just a pilot – a hot shot fighter pilot, a test pilot and maybe round out my career as an astronaut."

Frisbie earned his private pilot license as a student at the Greenville Airport during the summer before his senior year in high school.

"I wanted to fly – that was my main dream," he says.

However, Frisbie says that his instructor – Vern Johnson, who worked at the Greenville Airport – suggested that he should take a different approach.

"He explained to me that since Vietnam had just ended, the military had a mass exodus of pilots," he says. "Vern told me that the market for pilots was flooded. He suggested that I go to A&P (Airframe & Powerplant Program) school. He thought I could break through the back door as a pilot and a mechanic because employers looked for pilots who could do both jobs."

Frisbie graduated from Belding High School in 1973, and he enrolled at Montcalm Community College in the fall, where he earned his Aviation Maintenance Technology Certificate.

Although his life as a pilot has taken shape a little differently than his childhood dream, Frisbie says he made the right decision when he enrolled at MCC, and he credits the college for helping him achieve his dream.

He says he appreciates the quality of education he received at MCC and the resources the college provided for its aviation maintenance program.

"The instructors brought real world knowledge to the classroom," he says. "I thought they were top notch. They were highly experienced in their field."

Frisbie says the college had a "good sample of aircrafts to work on," including a jet and a crop duster.

"It was a great learning experience. There wasn't anything that we would see out in the field that we couldn't do. It was an excellent school," he says.

His experience in college helped shape his professional life. Throughout his career, Frisbie has worked as an A&P mechanic, a contracted pilot and staff pilot in private industry and as a commercial airline pilot.

"I still love airplanes and what I do for a living," Frisbie says.

Frisbie and his wife, Constance, live in Middleville. They have three children, Adam, Amanda and Austin.

A highlight of his career, he says, was the opportunity to fly with Adam at Expressjet, as captain and first officer, respectively. Frisbie says he hopes to someday have the opportunity to fly with Austin, too, who also works with Expressjet.

"I'm sure that flying with two sons at the same company is not one for the record books, but it sure is cool," Frisbie says.

(This cameo was originally published in 2013.)

Breann Gardner works with a team of professionals to guide development of television commercials, radio announcements and social media campaigns to bring brand awareness to customers.

The 22-year-old Hubbardston native works at Meijer with the brand development team as an agency project coordinator. There, she specializes in project management, working with top digital and creative agencies to develop a variety of Meijer's media images.

"I manage the relationships we have with our agencies, ensuring clear, daily communication," she says. It's a critical role in branding and marketing for the supermarket chain that boasts about 200 stores in Michigan, Illinois, Indiana, Ohio and Kentucky.

Gardner earned a Certificate in Liberal Studies with high honors from Montcalm Community College in May 2010 before transferring to Grand Valley State University where in 2012 she completed her Bachelor of Science degree in Advertising with an emphasis in public relations.

Gardner chose to attend MCC to complete many of her basic courses before transferring to a university. At MCC, she completed requirements for the Michigan Association of Collegiate Registrars and Admissions Officers (MACRAO) agreement, which grants smooth transfer of 30 credit hours of coursework to be applied toward a student's general education requirements at participating Michigan institutions.

"I wanted to attend a small, yet credible college, that was close to home before transferring to a university," Gardner says. "My experiences at MCC were great. The classroom sizes contributed to a healthy learning environment and the staff and professors were wonderful. They were truly engaged and wanted to help," she says. "I was able to get a great first year's education that prepared me for the larger university setting. MCC prepared me not only for a four-year university, it also helped me gain the knowledge and soft skills I needed to enter the workforce," Gardner adds.

While attending GVSU, Gardner served as president of the GVSU

Chapter of the Public Relations Student Society of America (PRSSA), Vice President of Operations for GrandPR, and was a communications intern at Amway in Ada, Mich.

"My year-long internship with Amway was amazing," Gardner says. "It helped me understand how a fast-paced global corporation operates – how to strategize and think big."

In addition to her position at Meijer, Gardner serves as the Vice President of Collegiate Relations on the board of the American Marketing Association (AMA) of West Michigan, where she works with student AMA chapters to help them create more engagement between the professionals and students.

"As a young professional myself, I believe students are the future, so it's important for them to have professional mentors they can look up to," she says.

In addition to her coursework at MCC, Gardner gained real-world interviewing, reporting and writing experience as a volunteer in the college's Communications Office.

"To this day, I use my press release examples that were published in newspapers as examples in my portfolio," she says. "MCC truly values education," Gardner adds. "The instructors, campus, classrooms and teaching techniques are truly state of the art. I was able to learn, gain knowledge, volunteer and make a difference all while attending MCC." Gardner and her husband, Ryan, reside near Lowell.

(This cameo was originally published in 2014.)

Paloma Ibarra-Ramírez found a fresh start at Montcalm Community College.

In 2008, she was attending college in her hometown of Torreón, Coahuila, Mexico, but she was discouraged.

"My voice had no value," she says. "I came from a family with many values that I try to follow every day. My parents have always told me that the only thing I'll be inheriting is my education, but the education wasn't meeting my expectations."

Ibarra-Ramírez said later that year she had the opportunity to travel to the United States with a tourist visa – a type of non-immigrant visa issued to individuals who are visiting the United States to engage in tourism – and she took it.

"My plan was to learn English and to get to know the area," Ibarra-Ramírez says. "I thought one of the best ways to accomplish these things would be to attend classes at a college or a university."

However, she soon learned that with a tourist visa, she could not enroll in classes to earn college credits. After meeting with representatives at several colleges, she says MCC's staff determined that she could take noncredit college courses without violating the terms of her visa. She enrolled at MCC in the fall of 2008.

"I spent many hours on campus learning English by taking guitar lessons, leadership workshops, meditation and other courses," she says. "The college gave me new options. I realized the educational quality MCC offers as well as the opportunities I could have if I were to study here in the United States. It was also the first time that I found myself surrounded by professors who cared and who listened to what I had to say."

Ibarra-Ramírez completed several noncredit classes before travelling back to Mexico to secure her resident card so she could return to MCC to finish what she started.

"The second time around I enrolled as a full-time student," she says.

Ibarra-Ramírez earned an associate degree in applied science in technical drafting and design from MCC, and transferred to Ferris State University where she received a bachelor's degree in product design engineering technology in 2013. She is now in her dream job as the associate program engineer at Cooper Standard Automotive.

She says MCC "changed my future. Since the beginning of my first semester, the professors and tutors not only taught me class material, they also taught me lifetime values based on their own life experiences.

"People at MCC welcomed me like family. Even though my home is many kilometers away, I found a second home at MCC," she says.

"MCC gave me opportunities to have experiences where I met people who stood by my side, guided me and taught me lessons – not just at an educational level, but also at a personal level," Ibarra-Ramírez says. "My teachers and tutors were always helpful to me and have supported my dreams and goals through my journey at MCC."

(This cameo was originally published in 2011.)

Erin Kitchenmaster says she had a "fantastic start" to her career as a student at Montcalm Community College. Kitchenmaster is a certified registered nurse anesthetist (CRNA) at William Beaumont Hospital in metropolitan Detroit. She says she enjoys working with a variety of patients and medical professionals. A typical day for her includes meeting with patients, determining anesthetic requirements based on their needs and the needs of the surgeon, checking the equipment she will use during the procedure and sedating and monitoring patients before, during and after their procedure.

During the two years she attended MCC, Kitchenmaster says she appreciated the friendly atmosphere and knowledgeable instructors.

"I loved the intimate size of MCC," she says. "The valuable education I received at MCC and the convenient location aided in my success."

Kitchenmaster earned an associate degree in nursing from MCC in 1995 and transferred to Northern Michigan University, where she completed a bachelor's degree in nursing in 1997. At that time, she worked as a registered nurse in a Surgical Intensive Care Unit at Spectrum Health – Butterworth Hospital in Grand Rapids, in preparation to pursue her master's degree to become a nurse anesthetist – a program that requires at least one year of critical care nursing experience.

In 2000, Kitchenmaster began a full-time graduate program at Oakland University in Rochester, Mich., where she earned a master's degree in nurse anesthesia in 2003.

Kitchenmaster says she chose nursing as her profession because of the versatility and challenges it offers.

"I enjoy variety, and in this profession, a person does not become bored. Anesthesia was my choice because I wanted to work in the operating room," she says. "Since hospitals operate 24/7, I'm able to work a varied schedule, which is convenient for me."

She says she balances her career, which is as emotionally draining as it is physically challenging, by enjoying down time on the beach and skiing "out West" and in the Austrian Alps.

Kitchenmaster also enjoys "giving back" to the community through charity work.

"I have volunteered on medical mission trips while taking vacation time by providing free anesthesia services to patients with limited access to health care in rural areas of both the Philippines and the Dominican Republic," she says. "It is common for people in these remote areas to rely exclusively on American medical services and to wait several years for surgery that would be attainable immediately in our country."

Kitchenmaster urges others to choose a program of study and give it their full attention.

"Choose something, anything to study, regardless of whether you know what you want to do in life," she says.

And, that's advice she backs up with another commitment. In 2004, Kitchenmaster established the MCC Foundation Erin Kae Kitchenmaster Scholarship. It annually awards $300 to a full-time single-parent student pursuing an associate degree in nursing.

(This cameo was originally published in 2011.)

Timothy Lindsey received more than an education at Montcalm Community College. The Lakeview-area resident says he also had a built-in support group while he battled Hodgkin's Lymphoma cancer.

The owner of Lindsey's Outdoor Preservations, a taxidermy, rustic furniture and décor shop in Lakeview, Lindsey says his fight against cancer prompted him to follow his lifelong dream of owning his own business.

Lindsey graduated from MCC in 2006 with an Associate in Applied Science degree in Criminal Justice. He then transferred to Ferris State University where he earned his Bachelor of Science degree in Criminal Justice in 2008. He also is a 2004 graduate of the Belding Police Reserve Academy.

A 2002 graduate of Greenville High School, Lindsey began college at MCC the fall after he completed high school. He was nearly done with classes at MCC when he was diagnosed with cancer, which dramatically changed his educational plans.

He says he was "set to transfer to Ferris and attend the police academy" when he was diagnosed with the disease in February 2005. Facing cancer treatment, he decided to further his studies in business at MCC instead of transferring. He underwent treatment until July 2006, when he was deemed "cancer free."

"MCC was a great experience," Lindsey says. "I had great professors who helped out while I underwent treatment for my cancer. I had one sweet instructor who always looked me up to see how I was doing," he says.

"MCC gave me a place where I could grow as an individual and educate myself," Lindsey says. "It also gave me something to keep my mind off of my cancer treatments.

At MCC, I gained the knowledge I needed to attend Ferris State University and to eventually start my own business. It was while I was attending MCC that I started to think about starting my own business and following my family's tradition of owning a successful business," Lindsey says.

"MCC is a great place to get your general studies done for a lot less money. Plus, you can almost finish a bachelor's degree while attending MCC," he adds.

The avid outdoorsman resides in Lakeview with his wife, Miranda. He spends much of his free time hunting, fishing, trapping and camping, and he is licensed as a taxidermist with the state of Michigan. He specializes in custom European skull mounts, custom handmade plaques, and custom furniture and décor.

Prior to opening Lindsey's Outdoor Preservations in March 2011, Lindsey worked for the state of Michigan as a Juvenile Justice Specialist and a Foster Care Specialist. He is a certified Regional Detention Support Services (RDSS) Secure Transporter and In-Home Detention worker with the state.

"I enjoy working with youths who are under county or state probation," he says. "I visit with juveniles in their homes where I talk with them to find out how they are doing with their daily life and school responsibilities and how well they are following their probation requirements."

Lindsey says he appreciates the support he has received and he enjoys helping others. He is completing the process to become a Big Brother with Big Brothers Big Sisters of Gratiot and Montcalm counties and says he looks forward to becoming a mentor for area youths through this program.

During his cancer ordeal, Lindsey says he learned to take life one day at a time and to "look at the big picture."

"No matter what life throws at you, you never know what you can do until you're faced with a life-altering experience," he says.

(This cameo was originally published in 2012.)

Sherry Meyer has been involved in animal agriculture since she was a child. She grew up on a family-owned and operated dairy farm near Stanton and now she and her husband, Paul Meyer, own and operate Roder-Dic Holsteins in Byron Center, Mich. They are highly-respected breeders in the state's Holstein, Jersey and Brown Swiss dairy cattle industries.

Meyer attended Montcalm Community College from 1987 through 1988, where she completed coursework to fulfill general education requirements as a transfer student to Michigan State University. She earned a Bachelor of Science degree in Animal Science from MSU in 1991.

"MCC provided a good educational foundation for me," Meyer says. "I was able to take classes to complete my basic requirements for a lot less money than it cost to finish my degree at MSU.

"I appreciated that I could live at home and continue working on the farm while I attended MCC," she says. "I enjoyed the atmosphere and small class sizes, especially after I transferred to MSU and ended up in an auditorium of 500 students for some of my classes."

Meyer has a longtime passion for working with animals. "The first milk was shipped from our family farm in May 1981, so you could say I grew up with cows," says Meyer, who was 12 years old at the time. "I always helped with chores and as I grew older, I assumed more and more responsibility for daily farm operations."

Upon graduation from MSU, Meyer returned to her family's farm, Strautz Holsteins, and entered into an informal farming partnership with her parents, Pat and Chuck Strautz. She and her mom worked together nearly every day completing the daily farming operations until Pat retired and Sherry left the farm in April 2008. While much of the herd was sold, Meyer and her husband moved animals from each of Strautz Holsteins' historic cow families to their farm in Byron Center, thus preserving the genetics they worked to build over a nearly 30-year timeframe.

Meyer says she and her husband enjoy improving animals in their herd by putting to work their knowledge of genetics to breed cows that are more appealing to the eye and have increased milk production traits. Their efforts have earned them hundreds of top placings at cattle shows throughout the state. In 2012, a heifer bred by Rod-er-Dic Holsteins placed fourth in the world at the World Dairy Expo in Madison, Wisconsin. "That was one of our most exciting moments," she says.

In 2008, Meyer earned the Michigan Holstein Association's Outstanding Young Breeder Award – the organization's highest honor – for her achievements as a top dairy cattle breeder in the state. She currently serves as vice president of the Michigan Holstein Association and in 2014, she became the first-ever female president of the organization. She also has served in several leadership roles with the Michigan Farm Bureau at both the county and state levels, and with the Montcalm County and Kent County 4-H programs.

Meyer says her education in animal science has contributed to her successes, and she is glad that MCC is adding some agricultural courses to its offerings.

"Agriculture is our state's No. 2 industry and it is imperative to the success of Montcalm County," she says. "I have long thought that agriculture should be front and center in our schools, and I'm glad that Montcalm Community College has added an animal science course to its curriculum that transfers to MSU."

(This cameo was originally published in 2012.)

Steve Russell has spent more than half of his life protecting the citizens of Montcalm County. He joined the Montcalm County Sheriff's Office in May 1982 as a deputy sheriff, and was promoted to sergeant in 1996 and to lieutenant in 2010.

As the law enforcement division commander, Russell is responsible for all of the law enforcement activities in the sheriff's office, including patrol, investigations and support services. He supervises five sergeants, who in turn supervise 22 deputies.

Russell says the diversity in his career combined with the opportunity to make a difference in people's lives have driven him in his profession.

"For over 30 years, I have been employed by the same department, yet I have done many different jobs. I've seen the very best and worst that society has to offer – all of this while residing and raising a family in a part of Michigan that is very nice to live in.

"Don't get me wrong, I've had moments when I thought there must be a better job out there. I've missed many family events, my kids' sports and school functions, and I've been in situations when I wondered if I would come out alive," he says. "But I wouldn't have it any other way because that is what the police do."

Russell began his law enforcement career as a military policeman with the United States Marine Corps. When he was discharged in 1977, he turned to Montcalm Community College for more education before transferring to Michigan State University in 1979.

He says his studies at MCC "totally prepared" him to transfer to MSU where he earned a bachelor's degree in criminal justice.

"My time at MCC absolutely contributed to my career success," Russell said. "It was because of the education I received there that I was ultimately accepted to MSU."

"As I look back on my two years at MCC, I consider them my best college years," he said. "MCC was a very personal experience with great interaction with the instructors."

Russell says Ken Smith, who served as an MCC natural sciences instructor for 40 years, "still ranks as the best teacher I've ever had.

"The early 1980s were not good economic times. Jobs, especially in law enforcement, were hard to find. College-educated police officers were not the norm that they are now, and I consider my education the key to why I was hired and excelled in this profession," Russell says.

During his nearly 30 years with the sheriff's office, Russell has covered a lot of territory. As a deputy, he primarily worked road patrol and for many summers he served as a marine patrol officer on area lakes. He also spent three years working undercover narcotics with the Central

Michigan Enforcement Team, taught through the D.A.R.E. (Drug Abuse Resistance Education) program in area schools for two years and was the chief firearms instructor for the county for more than 20 years. He has also taught boating safety and hunter safety classes at MCC.

"I speak to young people all the time and when I ask about their future plans, I often hear, 'I'm only going to MCC,'" he says. "Only MCC? MCC is the jewel of Montcalm County. It has started the career of many thousands of successful people over the years, and I count myself as one of them."

(This cameo was originally published in 2011.)

Sue Snyder never intended to open her own business. But, sometimes the best outcomes are unexpected.

Self-employed for 18 years as a piano teacher, Snyder says her first experience as a student at Montcalm Community College in the mid-1990s helped shape her career as a businesswoman and teacher, and brought her back to the college in 2006 when she decided to pursue her bachelor's degree in education.

Snyder earned an Associate of Liberal Studies degree from MCC in 1997. While attending the college she realized that much of her coursework was in the business field, but it wasn't really what she wanted to do.

"Once I got into the program, it was clear that I didn't want a business degree," she says. "Isn't that ironic, since I'm now a business owner?"

However, Snyder says the experiences she had as a student provided a background for her future in ways she never imagined.

At the time, she was teaching piano to a few students. One of Snyder's classes was Introduction to Business with the late Business Instructor Bob Campbell.

"We were walking down the hall, and jokingly I said, 'You know, I'm not going to go into business,'" Snyder says. "He smiled and told me that everything I was learning I would use with my piano instruction. He was right. I increased my number of piano students dramatically at that point. It wasn't so much what Bob said, but he confirmed my feelings about my piano business.

"I did use that degree," she adds. "It was kind of a turning point for me."

Snyder says that the relationships she had with her instructors at that time carried over when she returned to MCC 10 years later.

It was another turning point in Snyder's life. Her husband had been laid off from his job and Snyder had applied for several positions only to find that she was either over qualified or under qualified for the jobs. A natural educator, she says the time was right for her to return to college to pursue her teaching degree.

After having such a good experience at MCC years earlier, Snyder says going back to the college was a natural choice for her before transferring to Aquinas College, where she earned her bachelor's degree in education in 2008.

"There was no place else I would go. MCC was my first choice, and I still feel that way," she says. "I made good relationships with some instructors and they really were powerful influences. It's so positive when instructors invest in their students and really want to see them succeed."

Today, she continues to use her degree and the business acumen she has learned over the years as the owner and operator of Posey's Place, a high-quality, consignment store in Greenville that specializes in plus-size women's clothing and accessories, as well as teaching supplies, children's books and piano lessons. Named after her mother, who in retirement took on the character Posey the Clown, Snyder says the business is just another testament to the foundation she built through her college studies.

Snyder and her husband, Jeff, reside in Greenville. They have three children, one of whom attended MCC before graduating from Ferris State University

(This cameo was originally published in 2014.)

Katrina Soper is an artist, an educator and a leader. She recently wrapped up a busy year serving as Regional Vice President for the Michigan Region of the Phi Theta Kappa (PTK) Honor Society and was runner-up in her campaign for the organization's Division III International Vice President.

Soper grew up on a dairy farm in northern Wisconsin and, as a result, hard work was instilled in her at a young age. This value has driven her success personally and professionally. She graduated Cum Laude from Andrews University in 2006 with a Bachelor of Fine Arts Degree, with an emphasis in painting.

As her life changed, Soper returned to college to pursue a health-related career. She has completed nursing and allied health coursework at Montcalm Community College in preparation for the Radiography program at Mid Michigan Community College. Soper recently returned to MCC to earn an Associate of Science Degree and plans to continue her studies to become a physician's assistant.

"I chose MCC for the same reason many choose community college — it was close and it was affordable," Soper says. "I had already attended a four-year university, and I did not want to accumulate more student debt. Little did I know what I was getting myself into when I enrolled at MCC — that choice ended up being one of the best choices I have ever made.

"The instructors and staff at MCC taught me the most valuable lessons I have ever learned — that I could do anything if I put my mind to it and that I was the only one who could hold me back," Soper says.

"They taught me how to believe in myself. Once I did that, doors I never even knew existed were opened for me," she adds. "They were behind me supporting me with each new challenge I took on. Without MCC, I never would have learned the value of believing in myself or have had the support to surpass even my greatest expectations.

"The classes taught at MCC are equal to or surpass the quality of the ones I took at a four-year university," she says.

In addition to classroom instruction, Soper's involvement in MCC's Alpha Tau Alpha chapter of the PTK Honor Society has helped her learn communication and decision-making skills that will last a lifetime. She is putting them to work as a science tutor and a painter.

As a regional officer, Soper presided over all Michigan PTK chapters. In her bid for international office, she participated in interviews and presented a speech to an audience of 3,000 people.

"Phi Theta Kappa made me realize that outside my comfort zone is actually a pretty comfortable place," Soper says.

She adds that she has learned valuable life lessons during her college experience.

"Just because you are an honor student doesn't mean you have to succeed all the time. Some of our greatest lessons learned are found in failing," she says.

"The relationships I have built with the faculty and staff at MCC are unlike any other that I have had in my past academic experiences. They became more than just my instructors or advisors, they became my friends, making every experience at MCC one of my favorite experiences," she adds.

(This cameo was originally published in 2013.)

Thad Taylor has spent more than half of his life protecting citizens as a law enforcement official and now he is pursuing another passion – putting his experience to work as the Cedar Springs City Manager.

A Greenville native, Taylor took the helm in Cedar Springs in September 2012. His approach to public service is "my door is always open." His enthusiasm and commitment to his family, his career, and the people he works with and serves is a lesson Taylor says he learned early in life.

Taylor attended Montcalm Community College in 1974. Reflecting on the year he spent at the college, he recalls the mentoring he received from then Admissions Advisor Bob Minnick and says it has inspired him throughout his career.

"He was committed to the college, and he was committed to the kids and to education," Taylor says. "I got a front row seat at a very early age of what it means to be that committed and to have that kind of passion for something. That kind of focused me on the people that I wanted to work with. I wanted people who had that commitment and that passion."

It's a lesson he says he has remembered throughout his career.

Taylor served as a police officer and public safety sergeant for 11 years in Greenville before moving to Dewitt Charter Township in 1989 to become its Public Safety Director. In 1992, he and his family moved to Alpena where he served as the Public Safety Director for 16 years. In 2006, he assumed the joint role of Public Safety Director and City Manager and continued as City Manager from 2008 through 2012.

During his career, Taylor has served as a volunteer with a variety of local and state organizations including Michigan Chiefs of Police, Michigan Local Government Management Association, Michigan Municipal League and several others. He was also appointed to the Firefighter Training Council by former Governor John Engler.

Taylor says he is proud of the time he spent volunteering with Big Brothers Big Sisters of Michigan. Of all of the awards he has received during his career, he says being honored as the State of Michigan's Big Brother of the Year is his greatest accomplishment.

"What's most rewarding about that is to make a difference in a child's life," he says.

Looking back, Taylor has valued the life lessons he learned at MCC.

"The education at a community college is better than what you get someplace else," he says. "We had very small classes and there were a lot of life experiences that I couldn't have replicated at a university.

"I don't think that I would have been as successful at college if I had gone immediately to a four-year institution," he adds. "By going to MCC, I could focus on the difference in academic requirements between high school and college without the added pressure of the socialization skills that I would have needed to be successful.

"Years later, I think back and believe that attending MCC is the best thing that I could have done," he says.

Taylor and his wife, Theresa, have been married 34 years. They have two children. Their son, Ryan, is a police officer in Traverse City. Ryan and his wife, Gwen, have two daughters, Hailey and Olivia. Taylor's daughter, Jenna, and her husband, Trevor, live in Greenville with their three children, Jacob, Connor and Zach.

(This cameo was originally published in 2013.)

Top tier: Language Arts Instructor Jamie Hopkins and Social Science Instructor Kenric DeLong; Middle tier: Dean of Student and Enrollment Services Debra Alexander, and retired Administrative Assistant Jane LaLonde; Bottom tier: Adjunct Instructor Beverly Gates with adjunct colleagues James Nichols, Lester Albert, Christine Stander (also full-time support staff) and Vicky Wagner

Chapter 7

---•◆•---

Instructors, Leaders, and Staff

Throughout its 50 years, MCC has been pleased to have many talented, engaged, and faithful members on its faculty, administration and staff. These dedicated individuals have come from diverse backgrounds, various educational and professional fields, and complementary world-views. In 2015, MCC employed 29 full-time faculty members, 89 adjunct instructors, 28 full-time administrators, two part-time administrative staff members, 29 full-time support staff, and 73 part-time support staff members with 17 work-study personnel on its campuses and extension sites, under the guidance of its board of seven trustees. This chapter will highlight some representative members of the MCC family. Directories of all trustees, faculty members, administration and staff follow chapter 8.

Reflections of a Full-Time Instructor

Jamie Hopkins was an MCC student who later became a full-time English instructor. She joined the MCC faculty in August of 2011 after 13 years of teaching English at the high school level. She earned her undergraduate and graduate degrees at Central Michigan University. Literacy is her passion, and she currently works with underprepared college students, helping them strengthen their reading and writing skills for college success and completion. Her most recent project is researching and planning for a writing center on campus. Here are her reflections:

I see my time as a student at MCC as a series of snapshots in my memory.

One unforgettable snapshot is the sweeping view from the library that used to sit atop campus, occupying the top floor of the Administration Building. With a perch near the window, I could look out over much of campus as I used the technology of the time to search databases, locate cassettes to load into the computer, and print articles for research. With no Internet access in 1993-1995, the years I attended MCC, I spent hours in that library both researching and studying.

Of course, time in class fills many of my memories. I see a snapshot of Ken DeLong, head shaved, lecturing with his trademark animation under the fluorescent lights of Instruction East. My vantage point changed with my seating choice from one semester to the next. During most of my four semesters at MCC, I opted to sustain the workload that came along with Mr. DeLong's classes, knowing that the hours of study would pay off in learning and preparation for my next steps at the university.

In a snapshot from my last semester at MCC, I am packing up at the end of a class period after giving a graded presentation about Margaret Sanger supported by video clips recorded from a television movie. As I retrieved my VCR tape, Mr. DeLong, a master educator himself, approached me and asked if I was planning to become a teacher. I hesitantly replied, "Yes," since I hoped to continue my studies in secondary education with an English major. I sometimes wondered back then if I had what it would take to manage and inspire teenagers, but Mr. DeLong's reply was one that propelled me through three more years of college with certainty: "Good choice," he said.

Ken DeLong wasn't the only instructor who bolstered my confidence during those early years of my college education. I continued the habit of choosing instructors with a reputation for being tough and effective and signed up for multiple classes with Jim Fatka. My snapshots of his classes are varied, with students sometimes sitting in a circle discussing *Beowulf* or *The Canterbury Tales*, other times huddled around and considering a poster reproduction of a famous work of art. The most striking snapshot of all is the only one that I can still physically hold today, a note scrawled in his handwriting at the bottom of one of my essays. It says, "Worthy of an English major." Just as Mr. DeLong's words served as confirmation of my decision to pursue a degree in secondary education, Mr. Fatka affirmed my aspirations to major in English, the course of study I took up for both my undergraduate and graduate degrees. Mr. Fatka consistently challenged my thinking and writing, so his assessment of my abilities went a long way in convincing me that I could be successful in the English field.

Another flurry of snapshots comes to mind as I remember my semesters in Don Stearns' science courses. In one snapshot, we students tromp through the woods, led by Mr. Stearns as he taught us to identify trees and plants from their foliage and bark. In other snapshots, I'm in the science lab or completing my first oral exam. The final snapshot with Mr. Stearns is in Canada after he and his wife invited me and another student to travel with them and attend plays in Stratford. Each year they would generously offer this opportunity to a couple of MCC students. I still remember the plays, *The Pirates of Penzance* and Shakespeare's *Twelfth Night*. That this science instructor would see beyond my abilities in his courses and understand my passion for English is yet another testament to how MCC instructors take the time to not only teach students but to know them well.

So many instructors influenced my time at MCC, guiding that shy, recent high school graduate to the confidence of a college student ready to transfer to the university. After graduating summa cum laude from Central Michigan University with a degree in education, an English major, and physical science minor, I taught high school for thirteen years. Throughout those years, my students often voiced a desire to "go away" to college and follow their educational dreams at a university. I never hesitated to remind them of the quality, affordable educational opportunities available right here in Montcalm County. "MCC served me well," I assured them. Some of my most challenging college courses were the ones I took at MCC, and I was thoroughly prepared to transfer to a four-year college. As evidenced from all of the snapshots still stored in my memory, my instructors knew me, and with that knowledge, they guided me toward a successful career path.

After all of those years teaching at the local high school, I had the opportunity to return to MCC in 2011, this time as a faculty member. Some of those same instructors who once encouraged and inspired me are now my colleagues. Ken Delong's hair is longer and Jim Fatka's shirts are brighter, but they continue to set an example of caring commitment for their students, one that I hope I can live up to as well. Undoubtedly, MCC has changed and flourished. Our small community college has grown to include two campuses, several new buildings, and many renovations. Gone are the days of VCR tapes, televisions on carts, and limited computer access. Each classroom is now wired with the technology of the twenty-first century, and the college continues to strive for the best delivery of programs and instruction to ensure student success in a changing world. My work to help students build college-ready writing and reading skills in our zero-series courses is one such example of MCC's commitment to student success.

Together, my students and I are creating new snapshots for the future.

Adjunct Instructors

Since the beginning, MCC has employed part-time instructors to serve on its adjunct faculty. In fact, the first faculty was comprised of all adjuncts. But even with the establishment of its full-time faculty, adjunct instructors have been an integral part of the college's instructional team, teaching out of the fields of their expertise in which many still serve as practitioners. Today, MCC has 89 adjunct instructors who teach from one to three courses. A list of all the school's adjunct instructors with representative profiles is included after chapter 8. The following showcases MCC's veteran member of the adjunct faculty.

Bev Gates is the longest serving adjunct instructor at MCC, and serves as the president of MCC's Lifelong Learners. Here are her reflections:

> I was born and raised in Dearborn, Mich., and received my early education in the Dearborn Schools. In junior high school, I had a math teacher that made math

fun and he inspired me to teach math as my career. So I continued my studies at Henry Ford Community College, obtaining an associate degree in liberal arts, then continued on to the University of Michigan, Dearborn campus, to receive my bachelor's degree in education, with mathematics as my major and social science as my minor. While starting my first teaching job, I continued to work on my master's degree in math education which I achieved two years later.

My first teaching job was in the Dearborn schools, taking the place of the teacher that inspired me as he retired. After one year at Lowrey Junior High, I was transferred to Edsel Ford High School in Dearborn and I continued to teach there for four years.

It was during that time that I met the love of my life, Bruce. We married, then moved to Hanover Park, Ill., because of his work. I was lucky to find a teaching job immediately and worked for the Wheaton Public Schools for five years, teaching high school math.

City life became too fast for us and one weekend while visiting our Aunt and Uncle in Six Lakes, we talked, (they were realtors), and before we knew it, we made an offer to buy the Crystal Hardware in Crystal, Mich. We owned and operated the store from 1976-1991, seven days a week. During this time in 1987, I applied for a part-time teaching job at Montcalm Community College and began with night classes after my "hardware" day. I began in the summer, with summer school, after being away from teaching for 10 years. It felt great to be back to doing what I love.

I taught spring, summer and fall but eventually quit summer and regularly teach spring and fall up to the current time.

In 1987-2010 I became involved with Blue Lake Fine Arts International Music Exchange and hosted many European groups in our community for a few days, having concerts, planning activities, and finding host families for them to stay with. That also inspired me to host high school and college exchange students in my home for the school year and to work as a representative, finding host families for high school students. That International connection gave birth to the idea of a group from Montcalm County going to Europe.

So, in 1999, with the help and guidance of Lon Holton, I took a group of about 30 MCC students and community members on our first MCC international trip to Belgium where we stayed with host families, then we traveled to Paris and London, for a duration of more than two weeks. It was a great experience and we called ourselves World Wide Learners.

Other experiences at MCC, I have been involved every year with Santa's Super Sunday events since 1987, for a long time doing the craft area, now working with the clowns. I became an active member of Lifelong Learners and now find myself president of that group. I teach some non-credit classes, have taught a class on eating healthy and vegan, as well as crochet, fleece blankets, and other crafty things. I have also enjoyed helping at the MCC Let's Make a Deal sale.

My hobbies are gardening, golfing, and crafts of all kinds from stained glass to quilting. I will learn anything new, even rubber band bracelets.

Staff and Administration

According to retired staff member Lois Springsteen, "What makes MCC such a special place to work and learn is the family atmosphere. I think a large part of that is the spirit of the staff and administration. We have always been a team" (Springsteen, Oct. 24, 2014). "And the collective professional backgrounds of these individuals have served us well." The stories of long-time Administrative Assistant Jane LaLonde and Dean of Student and Enrollment Services Debra Alexander serve as examples.

Jane LaLonde is remembered by many as an administrative assistant at the college who served faithfully for 33 years. It was jokingly said by administrators and instructors, "We all know who really runs the college!" Here are LaLonde's reflections:

It started in 1978. I was divorced, without my three children, and living with my sister. She suggested I go to EightCAP to see if they could help me find a job. All I'd ever done to that point, while raising my kids, was bartend and waitress.

Even though the only office experience I had was a typing class I took for high school completion (with Pete Moutsatson as the teacher) ten years earlier, EightCAP suggested I apply at the College for one of the three secretarial positions available through the CETA work training program. Director of Personnel Lois Springsteen couldn't even consider me because she needed someone who knew shorthand. Director of Student Services Don Burns was not available to interview me because he was traveling in Spain. But Dean of Instruction Dennis Mulder, interviewed me and saw some potential. He hired me to assist the two full-time secretaries in the Instructional Office to meet the needs of three administrators and the entire faculty.

Then it seemed many things changed very quickly. One of the full-time secretaries in our office, Jill Pickens was given the position of manager of the new bookstore. Previously, selling textbooks had been a function of the library. At any rate, a new (trained and experienced) secretary was hired for our office. During her first three months, when the administrators went to a conference where registrations and hotel reservations were to have been made in advance and were not, she was asked to leave. I don't really know how many other disappointments led to that, I just know she was gone and the position posted again. I just stayed busy trying to keep up with the things that needed to be done.

Then one day as I was in the workroom running materials for instructors on the mimeograph machine, Director of Nursing JoAnn Regis came in and asked me to take the job. I was shocked and, of course, flattered, but told her I didn't think I knew enough to handle that responsibility. Her response was something to the effect that I certainly could handle it – I had been handling it for several months! Well, all of a sudden, I'm a full-time employee! I guess she was right. Surprisingly, my job didn't change that much from what I had been doing!

During another tumultuous time in my personal experience, the job kept going and growing. Secretarial responsibilities in the office had always been divided between Anne McCoy's liberal arts and my vocational education duties. Then, as a cost cutting measure, it was decided that our office didn't really need two full-time secretaries. Because I was involved with the department of education and board of nursing reporting, Anne, who had been at the College much longer than I, was given the choice of going on part-time or transferring to the personnel office. She took the position in the personnel office and, amazingly we still remained good friends.

Many of the liberal arts faculty were less than pleased about that change. They didn't believe a "vocey" (me) could understand their material and accommodate their needs. I guess I proved to them I could do it! Around that same time our director of occupational education left for other employment and the college created its very first vice president position who was also to take over occupational education duties. That made the new vice president, Don Burns, mine.

Of course I wasn't left alone with all these new and expanded responsibilities. We made use of what seemed to be a rapidly changing series of work-study students and even hired a few more people from that good old CETA work training program. Almost all of those CETA people went on to other rather important, good paying jobs after their CETA programs ended. I like to take some credit for that.

Fourteen years ago, my good friend Ken DeLong introduced me to theater. Before that, I had never even seen a live show. But, since I was Ken's go-to girl at work, he thought I could/would help him with a show he was directing for Bottom's Dream Theater/Flat River Community Players at MCC's Barn Theater. I did, and I was hooked. I've since done most of the backstage stuff for many productions, and even appeared in several of them. The only actual lead role I had was Mrs. Robinson in *The Graduate*.

And, I had thought I was afraid to be on stage – crazy. Theater created a sense of family much the same as the College did. It was also in that first production that I met my current husband, Emerson (Ric) Davenport.

As the years flew by I made so many good friends at MCC – and lost some good friends as well. I still miss Anne [McCoy] and J.C. [John Christiansen] so much and even feel a little guilty that I'm enjoying retirement as they should be.

I watched the College grow and change so drastically. I like to think that in my 33 years there, I helped make it happen. I truly feel so fortunate to have spent my work life at MCC. (LaLonde)

Debra Alexander is an example of what is possible at Montcalm Community College.

Alexander is MCC's Dean of Student & Enrollment Services. She originally came to the college as a student, and since then she has worked her way up to her current position.

"Honestly," Alexander said, "I received a schedule in the mail and realized MCC existed – prior to that I had never heard of MCC. I chose it because of its rural location and its homey feel."

Soon after she started classes, she realized how much MCC has to offer and now calls herself an "MCC cheerleader."

"With its low cost, rigorous academic experiences, lots of one-on-one assistance, small classrooms with caring, intelligent, helpful instructors, and a staff that *cares*, MCC opens the door for anything," she said.

As a student, Alexander realized her passion.

"I took an off-site class at the Ionia County National Bank in 1985, but didn't realize it was from a college. I just thought it was training through my employer. I took my first class in Sidney in 1990," she explained. "I had a *wonderful* English instructor who made me feel completely comfortable and made me realize that I would love education."

Following that passion, she came across a specific talent in one of her English classes.

"In my first class, English 100 (Freshman English), the instructor allowed me to work at an advanced pace. She apparently saw that I had potential, and graded my improvement as an individual, rather than along with the class," she said. "One of my papers was about catching a fish. She asked me to stay after class to let me know that, upon reading the paper, she thought

I had plagiarized from a professional writer. She read all of her husband's magazines to find out if it was a copy. It wasn't, of course. She shared her experience and concern as a compliment to my writing skills. I was so moved and felt so flattered! I still have that paper and will never forget that moment or that class."

Instead of unraveling under the false accusation, Alexander stood by her honesty and flair for writing. She allowed the incident to fuel her self- empowerment, realizing that with the right kind of determination and motivation, she could do anything – including getting over a dreaded fear.

"I hate math," Alexander said. "I was so bummed that I had to complete a math class to get a degree. I ended up with a fantastic instructor at MCC who made math enjoyable, and I ended up taking Trigonometry just for fun. It makes me laugh even today."

Alexander graduated from MCC with an Associate of Arts & Sciences in 1995 and an Associate of Business Administration in 1996.

Before leaving MCC, Alexander said she "met with an MCC Counselor, Bob Minnick (now retired) who was very kind and helpful. He helped me navigate the transfer process, and with his help I felt comfortable continuing onto Central Michigan University."

When she transferred to CMU, she still learned more about MCC.

"I found the courses at CMU to be *so* easy after MCC, which made me realize how rigorous the courses are here," she said.

Alexander graduated from CMU with a Bachelor of Science in Business Administration (Cum Laude) and a Master of Arts in Interpersonal & Public Communication.

After she completed her education, she worked for Mid-Michigan Industries for about a year before returning to MCC. In 2001, she joined the MCC Foundation as its Development Officer. In 2004, she moved to the college's Admissions Office, where she was responsible for admission policies, new student recruiting, new student orientation, middle and high school outreach, and student activities. In 2012, she assumed her current position of Dean of Student and Enrollment Services, where she is responsible for enrollment services, admissions' policies and procedures, as well as student conduct and advocacy.

"I love this place," Alexander explained. "I love how it provided me with an avenue into a new life and I love helping other students do that too. Everyone who works here is dedicated to serving students. I've never been happier." (Mack, Sep 2, 2014)

MCC's 50th anniversary picnic celebration with faculty,
staff, trustees and emeriti, August 22, 2014

Chapter 8

Celebrating a Legacy

Since its founding in 1965, more than 100,000 learners have passed through MCC's halls. In honor of these 50 years of faithful service to the Montcalm and surrounding community, President Bob Ferrentino declared the 2014-2015 academic year "a year of celebration for the MCC family and supporting friends." Frequent meetings of the 50th anniversary committee, chaired by Ferrentino, resulted in a myriad of campus-wide and community events throughout the year.

MCC's 50th Anniversary Picnic

MCC kicked off its "Creating Futures: Then, Now, Always" 50th anniversary celebration August, 22, 2014, with a picnic for its faculty, staff, trustees and retirees on the Sidney Campus.

Participants began the event while posing for a 50 formation photo next to the college's historic Heritage Village to commemorate the launch of the year-long celebration.

More than 100 celebrants gathered to enjoy fellowship, catered food, and a vocal music performance by Michigan recording artist Monique Doolittle.

"Our colleagues have helped make MCC the great place that it is," said Ferrentino. "As we embark on our golden anniversary, we wanted to celebrate the accomplishments of our first 50 years with our staff and faculty as we anticipate a year of celebrating with our community supporters as well."

Ferrentino said the college is looking forward to the next 50 years of serving the community.

"We will continue to partner with our communities to deliver on the value MCC provides, and to work with our business, industry and community leaders to provide the education and training needed to help our region continue to be economically prosperous," he said.

Gatherings, Banners, and Stories

During the 2014-2015 academic year and fall semester of 2015, MCC hosted community events, emeriti gatherings and historical celebrations. Anniversary banners designed by Creative Director Jody Butler were installed on lampposts throughout the Sidney and Greenville campuses.

August 25-28, 2014 welcomed students to campus with live music, refreshments, photo opportunities with the MCC Centurion (the present writer in costume), historical reflections, and a live, on-campus broadcast by WGLM-FM. A similar welcome week greeted students at both the Sidney and Greenville campuses during the start of the spring semester in January 2015.

Throughout the year, the college partnered with *The Daily News* to publish 50 stories for 50 years. The series highlighted MCC history, alumni and other topics relevant to the college. The stories were also posted on MCC's website.

"Music of the Seas"

A combined concert featured "Music of the Seas" on November 2, 2014, with a full MCC Alumni and Friends Choir and 55-member Philharmonic Orchestra, providing an allegory for MCC's historical journey. Held in the Activities Building Gym, the concert, directed by Valerie Vander Mark (vocal) and Jeff Ayres (instrumental), enjoyed a record attendance.

MCC's 50th Anniversary Week

March 2-5, 2015 was MCC's official 50th anniversary week, focusing on students and student celebrations. March 2, the actual birthday of the college, was celebrated with cake and punch, a performance by 2014 Miss Heartland Ashli Maser, a slide and video show written and narrated by Gary Hauck and produced by Betty-Jane Leeuw, and the assembly of a new time capsule with items contributed by the various student clubs and organizations. State Representative Rick Outman presented President Ferrentino with a "Special Tribute" from the State of Michigan, signed by Governor Rick Snyder, Senator Judy Emmons, and Outman. The tribute read:

> Let it be known that it is with great respect for the role that this outstanding school has played in educating our young people that we join the entire Montcalm community in marking the 50th anniversary of the founding of Montcalm Community College. On behalf of the countless students and families who have been touched by the work that has taken place here, we offer our thanks in celebrating this milestone ...

Ken Smith, composer of the music for the college's Alma Mater, led the staff ensemble and audience in the singing of the school song. Over 168 members of the campus family attended the event. March 3 and 4 continued student-led celebrations with live music and special events, and March 5 provided the culmination of the week's festivities with a noon and evening concert of the rock band Michael Locke and Repeat Offenders.

Anniversary Editions of the Ash Lectureship
In light of MCC's heritage rooted in 1965, three special speakers were selected for the 2015 February, April, and October Ash Lectureship Series to highlight America's relationship with Russia, the Space Program, and China.

The topic, "Russia: Then and Now," comparing 1965 with today, was addressed February 10 on MCC's Sidney campus by Matthew Rojansky, in partnership with the World Affairs Council of West Michigan.

Rojansky is an expert on U.S. relations with the states of the former Soviet Union, especially Russia, Ukraine, Belarus and Moldova. He has advised governments, intergovernmental organizations, and major private actors on conflict resolution and efforts to enhance shared security throughout the Euro-Atlantic and Eurasian region. Rojansky is the present Director of the Keenan Institute.

The April 22, 2015 Ash Lectureship featured NASA Astronaut, Dr. Andrew Feustal, speaking at both the Sidney and Greenville campuses on the topic, "America's Space Program: Then and Now." The noon presentation was held in conjunction with the annual student recognition luncheon, and saw a record attendance for that event.

Dr. Feustel served on the crew of STS-125, the final Space Shuttle mission to the Hubble Space Telescope. The mission successfully extended and improved the observatory's capabilities through 2014. In completing his first space mission, Feustel logged almost 13 days in space and a total of 20 hours and 58 minutes in three spacewalks.

The October 13 Ash Lectureship "China's World Influence – Past, Present, and Future" – by Dr. SuiWah Chan was presented at both the Sidney and Greenville campuses. Chan is a professor emeritus of Michigan State University and an associate of the Confucius Institute of University of Michigan. He teaches history of Chinese culture and lectures extensively on topics in Chinese writing.

Community Gala Celebration

A 50th Anniversary Gala Celebration featuring the combined choir and philharmonic orchestra provided for a community-wide celebration on April 19, with the historical presentation of Montcalm Community College's story in slides and video interspersed between the songs. Music of the 1960s, 1970s, 1980s, 1990s, and new millennium were selected by Choir Director Vander Mark and Philharmonic Director Ayres to represent the periods of the school's history. An audience of more than 400 enjoyed the celebration that featured cameo appearances by the college's first graduates, Tarry Stearns and Steve Foster, who recognized school founder Bill Seiter and first instructor Leslie Morford.

Retired Librarian John Carlson and Registrar Emeritus Sally Morais also shared their reflections and thanked Lois Springsteen and Don Burns for their roles in MCC's early history. Social Science Instructor Ken DeLong and Language Arts Director Jamie Hopkins discussed the eighties and nineties, and expressed appreciation to Vice President Jim Lantz and Creative Director Butler. President Emeritus Burns and Board Chairperson Karen Carbonelli reflected on the heritage of MCC's leadership, and President Ferrentino, Adjunct Instructor Debbie Bell and Student Ethan Vance addressed MCC today and in the days to come.

A highlight of the afternoon was the surprise announcement that two of the main campus buildings were being renamed that day in honor of Ken Smith and Leslie Morford. Near the end of the program, President Ferrentino walked over to where the two unsuspecting honorees were seated with their families, and presented them with the proclamation. In a news release for *The Daily New,* Samantha Mack recounts:

> Two buildings on Montcalm Community College's Sidney campus have been renamed to honor two retired instructors, as announced at MCC's 50th anniversary Community Celebration on April 19.
>
> Montcalm Community College's Instruction East Building and Instruction West Building were renamed in honor of MCC retired instructors Ken Smith and Les Morford.
>
> The Instruction West Building was renamed the Les Morford Instructional Building and the Instruction East Building was renamed the Kenneth J. Smith Instructional Building to honor years of distinguished service to the college.
>
> "In recognition of years of dedicated service to MCC and our students, the Board of Trustees approved our request to honor Les Morford and Ken Smith," MCC President Robert Ferrentino said. "From today forward, I am thrilled to announce that the Instruction West Building shall be known as the Les Morford Instructional Building and Instruction East

shall be known as the Kenneth J. Smith Instructional Building. These two gentlemen gave so much of themselves over the years, and their positive impact on the college has helped make us who we are today."

Ferrentino said that the idea to rename the Instruction West Building and the Instruction East Building after Morford and Smith, respectively, stemmed from their long-time commitment to help fulfill the college's mission of creating a learning community.

Morford was the first applicant to be an instructor at MCC. He served as a social science instructor for many years.

"Les has been highly engaged with MCC. The college and the community have reaped immeasurable benefit from this relationship," Ferrentino said.

He also worked with MCC's Lifelong Learners, served on the MCC Foundation Board of Directors and volunteered for Santa's Super Sunday, now called the MCC Holiday Celebration featuring Santa and Heritage Village.

"Les was one of the key people to get the college started," Board of Trustees Chairperson Karen Carbonelli said.

Smith served as a natural science instructor for many years, and after retirement, he served as a distinguished adjunct instructor.

"Ken epitomized MCC for the numerous students that he influenced in the classroom as an instructor. His positive influence on so many learners is evidenced by the tales of appreciation we hear from former students," Ferrentino said.

Smith established the college's first choir, the MCC choir, in 1967, which he directed for 13 years. He organized the MCC community band and wrote the music for MCC's Alma Mater.

"Les and Ken went way above and beyond while serving the college. Renaming Instruction West and Instruction East is the appropriate way to honor them and let them know that their dedication and skills are appreciated. They put their hearts into MCC," Carbonelli said. (Mack)

At the end of the program, Smith was asked to lead the audience in the singing of the Alma Mater, accompanied by the choir and philharmonic orchestra.

Anniversary Commencement

MCC awarded 361 degrees and certificates May 1 during its 48th annual commencement ceremony in the Central Montcalm High School gymnasium. To commemorate the event, trustees, administrators and faculty members wore a green and yellow sash bearing an embroidered 50th anniversary logo.

More than 100 candidates for degrees and certificates participated in the event.

Lt. Gov. and MCC alumnus Brian Calley and MCC student Rachel Gilbert addressed the graduates and their guests.

Calley was an MCC student dual enrolled at Ionia High School in 1994 and 1995. He earned a bachelor's degree in business administration from Michigan State University in 1998 and a Master of Business Administration from Grand Valley State University in 2000. He served Ionia as a community banker for 10 years then two terms in the House of Representatives prior to being elected with Governor Snyder in 2010. He is currently the youngest serving U.S. lieutenant governor.

Gilbert, of Trufant, earned a Licensed Practical Nurse certificate from MCC in 2014 and received an Associate of Science in Nursing during the commencement ceremony. At MCC she was a member of the Alpha Tau Alpha Chapter of the Phi Theta Kappa Honor Society.

During the ceremony, Calley was surprised to receive MCC's Associate of Arts degree, granted in a reverse transfer arrangement with MSU.

Chinese Exchange Program

Since several attempts were made over the years to provide a Chinese study abroad experience for MCC's students and faculty, administrators chose the anniversary year to finally include the realization of this dream. Thanks to the generosity of the MCC Foundation committee overseeing the Ash College Enhancement Fund, the dean of instruction's office was able to coordinate a trip at a cost for students not to exceed $2000.00.

MCC partnered with the Shandong Institute of Business and Technology in northeastern China for the trip in May 2015. This was the first study abroad trip offered by MCC that required participants to be enrolled in an academic study abroad course. Previously, anyone could travel without taking the coursework.

During the shared experience, Chinese instructors presented the history of China and Chinese culture, and MCC instructors and students explained Midwestern American culture, with emphases on humanities, social and environmental sciences. Students stayed in the college dorm, and were escorted on field trips to explore the sites of China.

The trip was facilitated by Social Science Instructor DeLong, Biology Instructor Heather Wesp, and Vander Mark (team leader). Vander Mark reported from the trip:

> Hello again from beautiful Yantai! The hits just keep on coming, with a beautiful surprise around every turn. Yesterday we visited the Yantai Museum and Yantai Hill, a gorgeous seaside park. I have attached some pictures, but they just plain don't do it justice. The Pagoda was just breathtaking, perched on a cliff above the Yellow Sea, and the group shot was taken with our new Chinese friends.
>
> Ken, Heather and I gave lectures to Chinese students. With our different subject matter, we covered a nice variety of ground, and the students seemed to enjoy our talks.
>
> We are most excited about the work that our students have done with the Chinese students, giving a

variety of presentations. It is gratifying to see the process they are going through in working with students from a different culture, and coming to some understanding about their similarities and differences. This has been an amazing experience, and everything we had hoped for. (VanderMark)

Looking Toward the Future

As MCC's celebration year continued, ongoing events, concerts, lectures, and presentations pointed back toward the school's heritage, and forward to its vision of the future. A 50th Anniversary Finale Concert was performed by MCC's philharmonic orchestra on November 8, 2015, much to the delight of a large and enthusiastic audience that gave a standing ovation. On the same date, the new time capsule was sealed and placed in the cabinet beneath "Crystal the Mastodon" in the college's library. And the legacy continues …

MCC Alumni and Friends Choir join the MCC Philharmonic Orchestra in a November 2014 concert celebrating MCC's 50th anniversary with Music of the Seas.

Top left: On March 2, 2015, State Representative Rick Outman presented MCC with a proclamation from the Governor's office. Top right: Dean Gary Hauck portrayed the MCC centurion. Middle: Instructor Emeritus Ken Smith led the staff ensemble and audience in the Alma Mater, which he composed nearly 50 years ago. Bottom: More than 160 members of the campus family came to enjoy the special presentations and program.

During the 50th Anniversary Community Celebration Gala on April 19, Emeritus Instructors Ken Smith (seated) and Les Morford (standing behind Smith) were honored by the naming of two campus buildings after them. The MCC Alumni and Friends Choir and Philharmonic presented music of the five decades, and MCC Student Ethan Vance and Emeritus President Don Burns shared reflections during the historical presentation.

NASA Astronaut Andrew Feustel talked about his in-space experiences during the spring 2015 Ash Lectureship and student recognition luncheon.

Alumnus Lt. Gov. Brian Calley gave the commencement address during MCC's 50th anniversary graduation program, and was awarded the Associate of Arts degree by reverse transfer.

MCC's 2015 study abroad exchange students and instructors along with their Chinese counterparts explored the sites of Yantai, China.

Top: MCC's first associate degree graduates, and first to graduate on campus in 1968: Helen Hamler, Steve Foster, and Tarry Stearns, standing with President Don Fink; Bottom: MCC's first associate degree graduates recreating the historical picture in 2015 with President Bob Ferrentino: Helen Hamler, Steve Foster, and Tarry (Stearns) Everingham

Top: Faculty members, administrators, trustees and emeriti assemble prior to MCC's 2014 commencement ceremony. Bottom: MCC faculty, 2014-2015

Directories

Trustees

Since March 2, 1965, MCC's Board of Trustees has been comprised of outstanding community leaders in business and education who are elected to provide oversight to the entire institution. In an effort to stay connected with all locales throughout the college's service area, the board has, from time-to-time, taken its meetings to the various communities served by the school. The trustees continue to provide fresh and relevant stewardship to the college and its stakeholders. In January 2015, the board was comprised of the following trustees.

Karen Carbonelli of Greenville joined the board in 1981. She served as trustee and treasurer until elected chairperson upon the retirement of Beatrice Doser. She graduated from Greenville High School, attended the University of Michigan, and became a licensed realtor in 1973. Carbonelli founded and managed Brandywine Realty, which was sold to Greenridge Realty in 2005. She continues on the staff of that firm.

Carol Deuling-Ravell of Sand Lake became a board member in 1999 and serves as secretary. She holds an MBA from Central Michigan University and an MA in educational technology from Michigan State University. She is a high school teacher.

Patricia Hinrichs of Trufant became a trustee in 2004. She is a retired Catholic Social Services program supervisor. Hinrichs earned her BS in education from the University of Wisconsin, and an MA from the University of Northern Colorado.

Joyce Kitchenmaster of Stanton joined the board in 2012. She received her BS degree in education and MA in health education from Central Michigan University. She served as an adjunct instructor at MCC from 1983 to 2004, and is co-owner of the Kitchenmaster Agency. She is also the president of the Association of Meemic Agents and is a member of the Sales Representative Policy Committee.

Robert Marston of Sheridan has served on the board of trustees for 26 years, has held the offices of secretary and treasurer, and is vice chairperson. He earned a BA and MA from Central Michigan University, and worked for 30 years as a counselor at Carson City-Crystal, Montcalm Area Intermediate, Central Montcalm and Greenville school districts.

Roger Thelen of Stanton joined the board in 2003, and holds the office of treasurer. He was a K-12 educator for more than 30 years, including 15 years as superintendent. He is the executive director of the United Way Montcalm-Ionia. He has a BS degree in education and an MA in administration from Central Michigan University.

Michael Williams of Sidney became a trustee in 2013. He received a BA in criminal justice from Michigan State University and is a graduate of the Oakland Police Academy. Hired by the Montcalm County Sheriff's Office in 1996 as a road patrol deputy sheriff, he served as a road patrol sergeant, and is now the undersheriff. Williams has been a member of the Central Montcalm Board of Education, the Montcalm County Police Officers' Association Executive Board, and the US Police Canine Association Region 19 Executive Board. He is president of the Montcalm County Command Officers' Association.

Former Trustees
(Name, Position, Total Years of Service)

MCC Foundation Directors 2015

Tom Kohn, MCCF President, Greenville

Wayne Korson, Canadian Lakes

Ransom Leppink, Lakeview

Dallas Lincoln, Lakeview

Cathy Mall, Rockford

Bob Marston, Sheridan

Rich Pease, Howard City

Karalyn Simon, Edmore

Todd Taylor, Greenville

Former MCC Foundation Directors

Stanley Ash	Karen Kehl
Ellen Baker	Ken Lehman
Tad Bartz	Betsy Leppink
Robert Brundage	Don McKenna
Mervin Bussell	Homer Miel
Stan Chase	Les Morford
Gary Copp	Robert Painter
Diana Crooks	Kathy Peasley
Jim Crosby	Mort Pomeroy
Beatrice Doser	John Reisner
Dean Eller	Lemont Renterghem
Sam Feravich	Judy Riessen
David Germain	Fran Rivard
George Gianacakos	Ron Story
Ralph Hauenstein	Herb Stoutenburg
Chuck Halterman	John Thorlund
Ted Hessler	Orville Trebian

Faculty 2014-2015

Don Adkison joined the MCC faculty in 2007, teaching college physics, introductory college physics, physical science, calculus, algebra, and trigonometry. He holds a BA in physics, math, and integrated science from Northwestern University, and an MS in physics from the University of Oregon. Prior to his time at Montcalm, Don taught at Lansing Community College, Delta College, and Kettering University. He identifies himself as "a Christian who thinks the Big Bang theory and evolution are reasonable scientific explanations for the mechanisms of creation, but humanity is the purpose of creation." His goals in teaching are to demonstrate a courageous and encouraging spirit, to help others think with precision and clarity, and facilitate discovery about the universe, humanity, and oneself.

Danielle Anderson first joined the MCC family in 2005, serving as adjunct and then as full-time instructor, from 2006 to 2012. From December 2012 to December of 2014, she was the clinical coordinator and educator for the Oak Hill Hospital in Spring Hill, Florida, and nurse manager for the Carson City Hospital. Anderson received her ADN from MCC, and holds both the BSN and MSN degrees from the University of Phoenix. She is pursuing doctoral studies at Walden University. Prior to her teaching at MCC, she had 14 years of experience on the nursing staff of the Gratiot Medical Center, and the Bayfront Medical Center of St. Petersburg, Florida.

Bill Bishop taught as an adjunct since 2004 and became a full-time instructor in 2013, teaching small business accounting, principles of accounting 1 & 2, tax accounting, computerized accounting, small business management, and legal environment of Business. He earned his BBA from Aquinas College, and MBA from Ferris State University. Bill also enjoys performing vocal and instrumental music and is a member of the American Accounting Association and the Institute of Management Accountants.

Dr. Joel R. Brouwer taught at Michigan State University, the University of Michigan – Flint Campus, Mott Community College, Jackson Community College, Unity Christian High School and Chicago Christian High School before entering the Montcalm Community College faculty in the fall of 1996. He earned a BA in English from Calvin College, an MA in English from Chicago State University, and PhD in English from Michigan State University. He teaches Freshman English 1 and 2, English literature, interpersonal communication, introduction to film, introduction to literature, and public speaking in addition to numerous electives. Dr. Brouwer taught high school English for twenty-one years, during which time he coached a state championship debate team and had numerous state tournament qualifiers in debate and forensics. He has written a newspaper film review column and has published numerous articles on various topics including film, television, culture and education.

Dr. James Brown began teaching full time at MCC in 1996. Prior to this, he taught at Grand Rapids Community College starting in 1986. He holds an AA from Grand Rapids Junior College, BA in human resources from Spring Arbor University, MS in information technology and resource management from Nova Southeastern University, and an EdD Western Michigan University. He also completed graduate studies post doctorate in educational technology from Columbia University. Besides teaching for MCC, Brown is a violinist in the Kent Philharmonic Orchestra, and plays bass, guitars, and synthesizer bass pedals in a progressive rock band and has played an upright bass both with the orchestra as well as a three-piece rockabilly band. Brown is also an artist and works in several media including oil, acrylic, and mixed media on canvas and paper, and in steel, creating larger sculptures and installations. The steel sculpture "Breaking Free of Cubism," installed on the MCC campus, was his 2013 ArtPrize competition piece in Grand Rapids. (He has successfully entered the ArtPrize competition for five years.)

Brandy Bunting is a Counselor at MCC and member of the full-time faculty. She came to MCC in the late 1990s as a student and returned in 2004 as an adjunct instructor and began as a part-time counselor in 2006. She received two full-time counselor appointments in 2008 and 2009, and was hired as a full-time faculty member in 2009. Her primary role is as a counselor, but she has also taught general psychology, sociology, social problems, introduction to social science and effective online learning. Bunting earned a BA in psychology and an MA in counseling from Michigan State University. In her free time, Bunting enjoys showing quarter horses on a national level. She has earned the titles of High Point All-Around Youth in the Nation, Reserve High Point All-Around Amateur in the Nation, Reserve World Champion, two-time National Champion and two time All American Quarter Horse Congress Champion.

Lisa Cogswell received her associate's degree in nursing from Montcalm Community College in 1999, and her BSN from Grand Valley State University in 2002. She is currently pursuing an MSN degree from Walden University. After receiving her LPN, Cogwell worked in long term care before transferring to Carson City Hospital. Upon completion of her ADN, she worked the next ten years at Carson City Hospital in the Pediatric and Medical-Surgical Unit. In 2001 she joined the MCC adjunct faculty, teaching nursing and allied health. Cogswell joined the fulltime faculty as an instructor in allied health in 2014.

Kenric DeLong teaches American political system, introduction to science 1 and 2, Michigan history, Native American history, U.S. history 1 and 2, and Indian cultures of North America in addition to several electives. DeLong became an MCC Instructor in August of 1977, and has a BA and MA in political science from Western Michigan University. He taught at Kalamazoo Valley Community College, Western Michigan University, and Alma College. DeLong extensively incorporates service-learning in his various courses, and facilitates a regular service-learning trip and project with Habitat for Humanity on the Cheyenne River Reservation in South Dakota. He has presented at the Oxford University Round Table in England, received numerous teaching awards, and was listed in Who's Who Among America's Teachers and Strathmore Who's Who Millennium Edition. He lived for four years in Argentina and has traveled to Mexico, Ecuador, Chile and the Czech Republic, and has served as president of the Montcalm Area Reading Council.

Kristen Diehl became a full-time faculty member in the fall of 2007, after working 10 years in the automotive industry in operations management (Delco Remy America and Wright Plastic Products). She earned a BS in small business management from Ferris State University, an MEd from Aquinas College, and completed 24 hours of MBA coursework at Walsh College. Kristen teaches business math, intro to HTML, office administration, introduction to business, and concepts of management. Diehl also serves as treasurer of the Montcalm County 4-H Council and is a 4-H Leader with the Winfield Hustler 4-H club.

Dr. Michelle Gibson began teaching biology at MCC in 1999. She was an adjunct at Lansing Community College and held a post-doctoral position at MSU the year prior to starting at MCC. She received her BS in microbiology at Northern Michigan University and MS and PhD at Michigan State University from the Department of Animal Science. Her research involved dietary regulation of lipogenic genes (fat genes). At MCC she has taught a variety of biology classes: microbiology, anatomy and physiology, general biology, college biology and animal science. She assists with the nature trails and is the faculty representative on the MCC Foundation Board. She initiated a "Dream Booklet" program for students and continues to support it. She is involved with Science Olympiad, 4-H and science fairs at local schools and enjoys farming, gardening and reading in her spare time.

Jamie Hopkins graduated from MCC and Central Michigan University with both her undergraduate and graduate degrees. She joined the faculty in August 2011 after teaching high school English for 13 years. (See more information in chapter 7.)

Carolyn Johnson began as a part-time instructor at MCC in the fall of 1996, and joined the full-time faculty in the spring of 1997.

She holds a BA in philosophy from Grand Valley State University, and completed graduate courses in humanities at Central Michigan University. Johnson teaches art for elementary teachers, drama as a performing art, drawing 1 and 2, humanities 1 and 2, western culture, and introduction to art. Johnson has been a professional artist/craftsperson since 1975. After working in two dimensional media, she created a business in three dimensional small sculpture and jewelry. She has done exhibitions, art fairs, and is represented in a number of galleries from Kansas City to New York City and Minneapolis to Miami. She led an MCC study-abroad trip to Paris, Rome, Florence and Pompey, co-facilitated a field trip to London, and participated in a cultural trip to Budapest, Bratislava, Vienna, Prague, Berlin, and Szczecin, Poland. She identifies herself as "a bleeding-heart liberal and a Macintosh computer fanatic."

Karen Lincoln became a full-time faculty member in January of 1988. Prior to her time at MCC, Lincoln taught science and health studies at Breckenridge elementary school for two and a half years, leaving to pursue a career in nursing. As a nurse, she taught childbirth classes and provided in-service education for the general nursing population and mentored new employees hired in the Maternity unit. She holds a BA in education and speech from Alma College, an ADN in Nursing from Mid-Michigan Community College, and an MSN in nursing education from Grand Valley State University. Lincoln teaches nutrition and diet therapy, maternal-child nursing, advanced nursing care of the childbearing family, maternal-child nursing, leadership, and body systems and disease. She also sings in a semi-professional trio called Trillium, and has performed in many musical theater productions with the Gratiot County Players.

Brianne Lodholtz became a full-time faculty member in 2011, after teaching as an adjunct and full-time temporary instructor at MCC, and at Grand Rapids Community College. She received her education at Grand Valley State University. Lodholtz teaches transitional mathematics.

Daniel Long earned a BA in mathematics, statistics and actuarial science and an MA in mathematics from Central Michigan University, and taught at Davenport University, Kirtland Community College and Central Michigan University before becoming an instructor at MCC in the fall of 1997. He teaches calculus 1 and 2, statistics, college algebra, trigonometry, and elementary algebra. Long enjoys several outdoor activities including hunting, fishing, hiking and carpentry work, and listens to music. He is a member of the Michigan Mathematical Association of Two Year Colleges (MichMATYC).

Beth Markham served as a member of the adjunct faculty for MCC from 2005 to 2008, and was appointed to the full-time faculty in 2008. Prior to coming to MCC, Markham served on the Per Diem Staff RN at Forest View Psychiatric Hospital, and Visiting Faculty for FSIL, Léogâne Haiti. Faculté des Sciences Infirmières de l'Université Episcopale d'Haïti in Léogâne (FSIL). Her specialty is psychiatric mental health nursing, for which she has been certified by the ANCC since 1986. She holds an RN diploma in nursing from Blodgett School of Nursing, a BSN from the University of Michigan, MSN from Walden University, and a Parish Nurse Certificate from Calvin College. She is a member of the American Psychiatric Nurse Association. One of Markham's objectives for MCC's nursing students is to assist them in learning how to be cultural sensitive in their nursing practice. She is a visiting instructor for a BSN school in Haiti, and emphasizes to her students that a health care professional is expected to be a life-long learner and increasing one's knowledge about culture is often self- directed.

Jan Roy began teaching at MCC in August, 1986. She has a BS degree with a major in mathematics and a minor in biology and a Master of Arts in education with an emphasis in secondary mathematics from Central Michigan University. She has taught every mathematics course offered at MCC, including some that are no longer offered. She received the Leslie K Morford Outstanding Faculty award in 1991 and 1999. Roy has served as President of the Michigan Mathematical Association of Two-Year Colleges and served on many committees within the organization. She is currently the Two-Year College Vice President of the Michigan Section of the Mathematics Association of America. Her most current professional interest is in the revision of mathematics education at all levels, K-16.

Michael Seaman has been a member of the MCC faculty since 1990, teaching macroeconomics, microeconomics, introduction to political science, social science 1 and 2, sociology, and indoor climbing. His education includes an AS from Jackson Community College, and a BA and MA in political science and economics from Central Michigan University. He is actively involved in a variety of aerobically-powered sports, including cross country and telemark skiing, road and mountain biking, backpacking, climbing and mountaineering.

Greta Skogseth entered MCC's instructional faculty in the fall of 2001, after teaching full-time as an English/speech instructor at Lincoln Trail Community College. She also taught at Central Michigan University, Delta Community College and Saginaw Valley State University, in addition to substitute teaching for Bay City Public Schools. She earned her BS in English and MA in English language and literature from Central Michigan University. Skogseth teaches freshman English 1 and 2, public speaking, children's literature and youth literature, and has been a pioneer of online education at MCC. She is the most recent recipient of the Leslie K Morford Outstanding Faculty Award.

Tore Skogseth worked in MCC's student services department from 2001-2005, was a counseling intern in 2006-2007, and joined the full-time faculty in 2010. Prior to coming to MCC, Tore (pronounced "Tudah" in Norwegian) served as a counselor at Grand Rapids Community College. He holds an AA from Lincoln Trail Community College, a BA in family life education from Spring Arbor University, and an MA in counseling from Spring Arbor University. In addition to counseling and caring for the college's special populations, Skogseth teaches college success, career development, and effective online learning. He also coordinates the general studies department.

Scott Smith, after receiving his AAS degree from MCC and BS in biology, chemistry and mathematics from Central Michigan University, worked as a senior technologist for a microbiology lab in Toledo. He taught chemistry at Fruitport High School for 11 years before coming to MCC. While working on his master's degree, Scott worked for the Amway Corporation as a guest researcher for two consecutive summers, working with supercritical fluid technology and method development for assaying the amino acid Taurine. He earned an MA in chemical education from Western Michigan University and joined the MCC faculty in 1999. Smith received Outstanding Faculty awards, and is a long-standing member of the American Chemical Society. He teaches algebra, introductory chemistry, college chemistry, and physical science, and participates in MCC's music programs as a guitarist and vocalist. He is the son of retired MCC Science Instructor and Music Director Ken Smith.

Jessica Snyder is a psychology instructor at MCC. She joined the college in August 1999 straight out of graduate school. She teaches general psychology, child psychology, abnormal psychology, psychology of sex & gender and early childhood development classes. She is also a co-advisor for MCC's Alpha Tau Alpha chapter of the Phi Theta Kappa Honor Society, and a co-chair of the assessment committee. Snyder earned a BA in psychology in 1990 and an MS in educational psychology in 1995, both from the University of Wisconsin-Madison.

Valerie Vander Mark began as a part-time instructor at MCC in 1989, and joined the full-time faculty in 1991. Val earned her BA in voice from the University of Michigan and MA in music education and supervision from Central Michigan University. She teaches choir, humanities, western culture, music appreciation, music in the elementary classroom, music fundamentals, and voice improvement. Vander Mark has been active for many years in community theater including the Flat River Community Players and Bottom's Dream Theater. She had leading roles as Maria in "West Side Story," Nellie in "South Pacific," and twice as Golde in "Fiddler on the Roof." She wrote the original music for "The

Treasure Tree," and several other compositions. In addition to teaching credit courses at MCC, she orchestrates on-campus music activities including the fall and spring concerts of the MCC Alumni and Friends choir, madrigal dinner, annual recital, and elementary music festival. She co-led the college's study-abroad trip to Rome, Paris, Florence and Pompeii, and facilitated the study abroad in London, England.

Chad Walden joined MCC's full-time faculty in fall 2014. He enrolled as a student at MCC in 1994, and completed the BS in education degree at Central Michigan University in 1999. He taught English at Central Montcalm High School and advised the yearbook for nine years before taking a position at Fulton High School. While at Fulton, he completed the MA in English language and literature at CMU. Walden later became a fellow of the Crossroads Writing Project, a site of the National Writing Project hosted by Ferris State University, and began teaching as an adjunct instructor at MCC in the summer of 2007. Walden has coached boys' and girls' basketball on various levels, and plays drums for his church's worship team.

Heather Wesp joined the faculty in the fall of 2003, after teaching at Hope College, Northern Arizona University, and Lansing Community College. She holds a BS in biology from Hope College, and an MS in animal behavior and morphology from Northern Arizona University. Wesp teaches biological science, zoology, college biology 1 and 2, anatomy and physiology 1, nature study, and undergraduate research. She is a member of the Michigan Community College Biologist and Association for Biology Laboratory Education. She has volunteered commitments to the Science Olympiad and Emergency Animal Rescue Center, and has directed the MCC Science Camp for 3rd-8th graders for many years. She has also participated in study-abroad field trips, including the Galapagos Islands.

Early College Faculty

Melissa Ausua joined MCC's Early College and adjunct faculties in 2013, teaching English. Before coming to the college, she taught middle school in Hawaii and Grand Rapids. She graduated from Grand Valley State University with a BA degree in secondary English education, and earned her MA in literacy studies and reading specialist certification at Western Michigan University.

Dean Gage is in his second year on the Early College faculty at MCC and also serves as adjunct, teaching social science. He has a BS from Grand Valley State University and an MEd from Ferris State University, with majors in public administration, social studies, and business education. He also holds an occupational certificate in vocational and technical education to teach construction and related classes. Gage is a member of the Michigan Construction Teachers Association and the Michigan Council for the Social Studies.

Patricia Yonker became the Early College instructor of math and science in 2013. She holds a BA degree *summa cum laude* in secondary math and science education from Cornerstone University. Prior to her service at MCC, she taught secondary math and science at Barry County Christian School and served as a substitute teacher and instructional consultant.

Former Faculty
(Name, Degree, Discipline, Total Years of Service)

Tracy Alberta, MSN, Nursing, 2

Donovan Anderson, MA, COPE, 4

Jean Bailey, MA, Computer Information Systems, 4

Wilma Baldwin, BSEd, Office Systems, 2

Elizabeth Bell, MA, Language Arts, 1

William Bezemek, BA, Business Data Processing, 5

Donald Binder, BA, Business Data Processing, 4

Vernon Blake, MA, Language Arts, 15

Helen Brehm, MA, Business, 5

Jane Bucholtz, RN, Nursing, 8

Gordon Burns, Vocational Certificate, 1

Donald Burns, PhD, Counselor, 3

Robert Campbell, MS, Business, 26

Earl Christensen, BSEE, Business Data Processing, 14

Anne Collins, BSN, Nursing, 2

Jennifer Cook, BSN, Nursing, 2

John Dargitz, BS, Drafting Technology (8), 23

Gordon Darrah, MBA, Counselor, 2

Lavonna Decker, BS, Nursing, 19

Allen Delamater, Industrial Technology, 3

Mary DeVos, MA, Nursing, 6

Richard Diehl, BA, Mathematics, 1

Kendall Downing, MA, Counselor, 1

Lillian Downing, MA, Counselor, 8

Edna Dyer, RN, Nursing, 2

Amy Eady, MS, Allied Health, 10

Gayle Ewing, EdS, Counselor, 5

James Fatka, MA, Language Arts, 26

Lisa Firestone, BS, Office Systems, 4

Frank Fishell, PhD, Mathematics, 19

Ipha Fishell, RN, Nursing, 2

Edwin Fogarty, MA, Physics/ Mathematics, 6

Charlotte Fokens, PhD, Counselor, 18

Richard Fox, BS, Automotive Mechanics, 25

Jesse Fox, MA, Aviation, 8

Nancy Fox, MA, Art, 16

Gerald Freid, MA, Social Science, 11

Barbara Goretzka, MA, Language Arts, 2

Robert Gravelle, MA, Counselor, 1

Jenny Griffiths, MSN, Nursing, 6

Eric Guenther, Vocational Certificate, 1

Danny Herman, MA, COPE, 1

Julie Hess, MS, Mathematics, 3

Marjorie Highfield, MA, Language Arts, 7

Christina Hollenbeck, MA, Industrial/Manufacturing Technology, 4

Herbert Hood, MBA, Business, 18

Bruce Hoople, BA, Automotive Mechanics, 2

Janis Hoople, MA, CIS Lab Coordinator, 6

Frederick Hop, MA, Drafting/ Construction, 7

Bruce Howard, MA, Data Processing/Mathematics, 2

Linda Hughes-Kilborn, BA, Counselor, 5

Marilyn Hummel, MA, Nursing, 8

Darwin Jensen, Vocational Certificate, 1

Norman Kanagur, BA, Food Services Technology, 3

Marc LaBeau, MS, Natural Science, 2

Ronald Lada, MA, Social Science, 4

Brenda Larsen, BSN, Nursing, 6

Harold Lee, BA, Language Arts/ Humanities, 2

Lawrence LeGree, BS, Automotive Mechanics, 28

Arthur Leinberger, BS, Automotive Mechanics, 1

Karen Lincoln, MSN, Nursing, 27

James Lucka, MA, Counselor, 34

Carl Maurer, BS, Automotive Mechanics, 2

Marla McClung, MSN, Nursing, 2

Roy Merrett, Vocational Certificate, 1

Larissa Miller, BSN., Nursing, 2

Robert Minnick, MA, Counselor, 22

Gary Moore, MA, Automotive Mechanics, 2

Leslie Morford, MA, Social Science, 19

Peter Moutsatson, MA, Business, 33

Betha Mowatt, MSN, Health Occupations, 15

Dennis Mulder, MA, Language Arts, 6

Kristine Mullendore, BS, Criminal Justice, 6

Sylvia Mustonen, BA, Language Arts, 2

Dennis Nelson, MA, Social Science, 31

Kathleen O'Connell, BA, Business, 3

John Pastoor, BA, Language Arts, 28

James Peacock, MA, Criminal Justice, 25

Gordon Peltier, Automotive Mechanics, 5

Larry Peterson, BA, Physical Education, 3

Ray Povolo, MA, Blue Print Reading, 1

Heinz Radtke, Welding, 9

JoAnn Regis, BS, Nursing, 5

Mary Rhoads, MA, Humanities, 1

Ruth Rose, RN, Nursing, 19

John Scheufler, MS, Natural Science, 2

Howard Seeburger, MA, Mathematics, 1

Beth Sendre, BSN., Nursing, 4

Kenneth Smith, MA, Natural Science, 28

Daniel Snook, MA, Developmental Education, 28

Robert Spohr, MA, Business Administration, 2

Donald Stearns, MS, Natural Science, 20

Maron Stewart, MS, Natural Science, 14

Sydney Swanton, MA, Mathematics and Industrial Physics, 1

John Twork, BS, Industrial Apprenticeships 1

David VanderArk, BSN, Nursing, 1

Joanne Walden, BA, Computer Information Systems, 30

Jerry White, MA, Humanities, 9

Marilyn Witter, RN, Nursing, 17

Leard Wylie, BS, Aircraft Maintenance, 9

Faculty Award Recipients

Master Teacher Award

1974, Kenneth Smith, Science

1976, Leslie Morford, Social Science

1978, Ruth Rose, Nursing

1979, Nancy Fox, Art

1979, Jesse Fox, Aviation

1980, Mary DeVos, Nursing

Outstanding Faculty Award

1981, Peter Moutsatson, Business

1982, Joanne Walden, Office Education

1983, Daniel Snook, Developmental Studies

1984, Leslie Morford, Social Science

1984, Kenneth Smith, Science

1985, Kenric DeLong, Social Science

1986, Earl Christensen, Business Data Processing

Leslie K. Morford Faculty Recognition Award

1990, Leslie Morford, Social Science

1991, Janice Roy, Mathematics

1992, Karen Lincoln, Nursing

1993, Jim Fatka, Language Arts

1994, Nancy Fox, Art

1995, Robert Campbell, Business

1996, Joanne Walden, Office Education

1997, Valerie Vander Mark, Performing Arts (Music)

1998, Marilyn Witter, Nursing

1999, Janice Roy, Mathematics

2000, Joel Brouwer, Language Arts

2001, Kenric DeLong, Social Science

2002, Charlotte Fokens, Counseling

2003, James Peacock, Criminal Justice

2004, Michelle Gibson, Biology

2005, Valerie Vander Mark, Performing Arts (Music)

2006, Scott Smith, Chemistry

2007, Joel Brouwer, Language Arts

2008, Kenric DeLong, Social Science

2009, Karen Lincoln, Nursing

2010, Danielle Anderson, Nursing

2011, Heather Wesp, Biology

2012, Carolyn Johnson, Visual Arts

2013 (In Memoriam), Robert Campbell, Business

2014, Greta Skogseth, Language Arts/Humanities

2015, Jessica Snyder, Psychology

Adjunct Faculty Representative Profiles

Debbie Bell is a graduate of Kendall College of Art & Design. She has been teaching art since 2001 for ages five to 95, and for MCC since 2005. Currently Bell is director and curator for the Belding Art Council and teaches a variety of art classes for the East Grand Rapids Recreation Center. *Artfully Yours* is a monthly paint bar which Bell presents at the Greenville Community Center. She has created commissioned art for area businesses, illustrated children's books, and custom design cakes.

Some of her art recognition awards include those from the Michigan Regional Visual Art Show; MCC Create Administrators Choice Award; and the Danish Festival Mural Award (2011). Bell's most recent exhibits (within past year) include: Art Prize "Listen to the Art" performances with St. Cecilia Orchestra at the Music Society; fine art performance art for Hark-Up concerts at the Devos Auditorium; and solo exhibits at Grand Rapids venues including One Trick Pony.

Brian K. Blomstrom (BS, Lake Superior State University, MPA, Grand Valley State University) has served on MCC's adjunct faculty since January of 2008; he instructs police administration & operations and criminal investigation. Blomstrom is a sergeant with the City of Greenville Department of Public Safety, is a nationally designated chief training officer and chief fire officer through the Center for Public Safety Excellence, and was one of the 2009 recipients of the Arson Investigator of the Year award through the Michigan Arson Prevention Committee. Governor Rick Snyder appointed Blomstrom to the Michigan Fire Fighters Training Council in 2011.

Dr. Lance Miller has been teaching for MCC since 1997. He also currently teaches for Grand Valley State University and Central Michigan University, and has been teaching at the college level since 1987. His courses include: philosophy, bioethics, world religions, and Social Sciences. Lance received his PhD from Michigan State University, an MA from Boston University, (including transfer graduate credits from Harvard University) and a BA from the University of Michigan.

Larry Moss, adjunct instructor of English and communications, earned a BA degree in theatre from Columbia College in 1986, after having studied music at St. Clair County Community College, and acting in the BFA program at Goodman School of Drama at DePaul University. In 2001, he enrolled in the graduate teacher certification program at Grand Valley State University and received his Michigan teacher's certificate in 2003, after completing an additional major in English, with a minor in history from the undergraduate program.

Since starting as an adjunct at MCC in 2004, Moss has taught English, communications, and philosophy. Moss has been involved in many activities at MCC, including the MCC Alumni and Friends choir, performing in the *Messiah*, as well as frequent appearances in the annual fall and spring concerts and the annual student/staff recitals. He is also a founding member of the MCC philharmonic orchestra, playing bass trumpet. Moss was Greenville co-chair of the Headlee override campaign.

Moss is a 2008 graduate of the Leadership Montcalm program, where he developed his final presentation, "The (Hidden) Art of Montcalm County," which he has expanded and presented to more than 25 audiences throughout Montcalm County over the past six years. The presentation covers the history and scope of arts and cultural activities in Montcalm County. In conjunction with Dr. Gary Hauck, Moss helped to establish the Montcalm Area Humanities Council, with the purpose of promoting and encouraging the arts and culture of our area. He has served as vice chair and chair of the MAHC. Larry has been published twice in *Michigan History* magazine, with articles, "Bert Silver and His Entertaining Family" (May/June 2013) and "Bell Ringer" (November/December 2014).

Moss has also been very involved in the greater community, as a church leader, Boy Scout and Girl Scout volunteer, and performer in Broadway Delights, Spectrum of Stars and the OUR3 Campaign annual fundraisers. Moss has also worked with students at Greenville High School, as Drama Club advisor and director and stage manager for several high school plays, and served, with his wife, Susan, as co-president of Greenville band boosters. He has served as a board member, vice president and president of the Flat River Community Players, as well as serving on the board of the Greenville Area Community Center, and as vice chair of the Montcalm Area Transportation Authority. He serves on the MCACA minigrant panel for region 4B. He has been elected twice to the Greenville city council, where he has served since 2007.

Jamey Nichols (BRE--Cornerstone University, MA--Western Michigan University, PhD candidate, Trinity Theological Seminary) joined the MCC adjunct faculty in 2007, instructing courses in psychology and communications. He also serves as senior pastor of Stanton's First Congregational Church, and was host of the Hope of Glory radio program from 2009-2011 and an editor and contributor to *Encompass Magazine* from 2007-2012. He has published numerous articles on faith, culture and politics.

Jim Peacock came to MCC in1985 as a part-time instructor teaching in the COPE prison program. He became the full-time criminal justice coordinator in 1986 and joined the regular full-time faculty in 1988, teaching criminal justice, physical education, judo, self-defense, psychology, humanities, and Michigan history. After retiring in 2012, Peacock remained as an adjunct instructor of welding. He is a member of the American Welding Society, and serves on the college's welding advisory committee. His education includes a BS in criminal justice (with honors), and an MS in criminal justice, both from Michigan State University. Prior to his arrival at MCC, Peacock served as an officer in the United States Marine Corps, and a police officer in Atlanta, GA.

Brooke Roman (BS and MS, Michigan State University) has served on MCC's adjunct faculty since January of 2013. She teaches anatomy and physiology courses. Roman is a member of the Michigan Community College Biologist group. She is the author of, "Short-term supplementation with active hexose correlated compound improves the antibody response to influenza B vaccine" published in Nutrition Research journal in 2012. She also works as an associate research scientist at a Biotechnology company.

Sally Spry is a part-time business instructor at MCC, which includes remaining up-to-date with ever-changing business data in the "real" world. She is also an instructor for the Michigan Department of Corrections in Carson City and previously worked in the Deerfield Correctional Facility. Spry earned two AS degrees in accounting and business administration from MCC in 1989, two BS degrees in accounting and business administration from Aquinas College in 1991, and an MS in accounting in 1993, with a specialization in Taxation.

Dave VanderSchuur received a bachelor of philosophy degree from Grand Valley State University with a double major in Spanish and theatre and a minor in English, and his MA from Michigan State University. He taught a variety of language arts classes at Central Montcalm High School for 29 years and began teaching at MCC in the fall of 2009. He reflects,

> I love to travel and learn about people and their cultures, particularly Spanish speaking countries, although I have also been to China, Australia, Israel, Guinea, New Zealand, and other countries.
>
> I live on a hobby farm (40 acres) approximately one mile south of MCC as the crow flies. I enjoy hiking, reading great literature, and being active in my church, First Congregational Church of Stanton. I went on my first build with Habitat for Humanity in Chile in January of 2014, and on my second to Nicaragua in February of 2015.

Vicky Wagner has been teaching early childhood education classes at MCC for 15 years. Additionally, she has worked as the Ionia County representative for Kent Regional 4C, in preschool – sixth grade classrooms, and has written the curriculum for and taught parenting education classes in the Youth Offender Program of the Michigan Department of Corrections.

Wagner has a master of education degree from Aquinas College, is a certified teacher and continues to do postgraduate work in the areas of early childhood education, learning disabilities and educational psychology.

Advocating for children, families and the community has been a lifelong passion for Wagner. She has served as: president/representative to State of Michigan for the Flat River Chapter of the Association for the Education of Young Children; board member of Ionia County Great Start Collaborative, chairperson of the Great Start Child Care/ Early Education Committee; board member of Ionia County Early On

Local Interagency Coordinating Council; member of the Montcalm Community College/Montcalm Area Career Center Early Childhood Advisory Board; board member of Montcalm County We Care for Kids Council and member of Ionia County Literacy Council. In her leisure time Wagner enjoys time with family, reading, bicycling, and sailing.

Karl Yoder (AA, BA, MMin - Bethel College, IN) has served on MCC's adjunct faculty since fall 2010. He has taught concepts of management, introduction to business, employability skills, and business English. Yoder has taught at, and was business manager for, Kentucky Mountain Bible College. He is the community reinvestment act coordinator for the north region of Chemical Bank. He serves as a city commissioner and is on the planning board of the City of Stanton, and is pastor of Mud Lake Community Missionary Church. He also serves on the board of the Michigan Missionary Loans and Investments, Inc.

Adjunct Faculty Members
(Name, Degree, Discipline, Years of Service)

Michael Adams, MBA, Accounting, 6

Philip Adler, MA, Allied Health, 1

Melissa Aususa, MA, Language Arts, 2

Jeremy Ball, MA, Computer Information Systems, 1

Kimberly Bell, MA, Language Arts, 6

Mike Blount, Industrial Technology, 2

Douglas Brown, AA, Auto, 9

Nancy Bruinsma, MA, 2

Donald Buchanan, M.A., Science, 1

Lisa Burggren, BA, Biology, 5

Jody Butler, BA, Computer Information Systems, 8

Frederick BW' Ombongi, MA, Business, 2

Robert Byram, MBA, Business, 3

James Cain, MSW, Criminal Justice, 3

Randy Cairns, Technical Drafting and Design, 7

Sally Carlson, MA, Business/Computer Information Systems, 8

Ronald Carlton, MA, Mathematics, 11

Amyee Carson, MSW, Criminal Justice, 6

Melissa Christensen, BS, General Studies, 2

Shari Ciganik, EdD, Mathematics/Computer Information Systems, 10

Anita Clark, Allied Health, BS, 8

Mary Ellen Cleary, Psychology, MA, 3

Kelly Coe-Decker, Nursing, MSN, 2

Lisa Cogswell, BSN, Nursing, 13

Leigha Compson, MA, Psychology/Sociology, 1

Jennifer Cook, BSN, Nursing, 10

Randall Cook, MA, Chemistry, 17

Elizabeth Crider, BSN, Nursing, 20

Cynthia Cuffman, BS, Computer Information Systems, 1

Timothy Cuffman, MA, Philosophy, 1

Jeffrey Cummings, MBA, Management/Marketing, 5

Cassandra Davis, BA, Mathematics, 8

Kelly DeLong, BA, History/Anthropology, 8

Allen Demorest, BBA, YOP/Business, 16

Norman Denny, AAS, Technical Drafting and Design, 4

Dana Desgranges, MA, Early Childhood Development, 1

Sandra DeYoung, MA, Science 1

Brittany Dillon, MA, Language Arts, 1

Michael Dodge, MA, Social Science, 2

R. Wayne Downing, MBA, Business/Computer Information Systems, 4

Amy Eady, MS, Allied Health, 10

Kris Eggleston, AA, Allied Health, 2

Sidney Ehlert, MS, Electronics, 37

Paula Ellsworth, BSN, Nursing, 3

Amanda Estill-Lofts, BS, General Studies, 1

Pius Ezeh, MA, Business, 2

Linda Ferguson, MA, Communications, 6

Thomas Ferguson, MA, Language Arts, 1

Robert Ferrentino, JD, Business, 1

Monica Frees, MA, Language Arts, 3

Dean Gage, MEd, Social Science, 3

Lisa Gardner, BBA, Computer Information Systems, 2

Beverly Gates, MA, Mathematics, 28

Brian Gavenda, BS, Mathematics, 2

George Germain, BS, Mathematics/Business, 17

David Gibson, BA, History, 4

Jessica Gilbertson, BA, Biology/General Studies, 5

Richard Sam Glaves, Biology, MS, 1

Carolyn Gleason, BS, Mathematics, 2

William Golombisky, MA, Physical Education, 27

Kurt Goodman, Welding, 3

John Goudzwaard, Business Administration

Alicia Haley, MS, Language Arts, 2

Susan Hatto, MA, General Studies, 5

Gary Hauck, PhD, Humanities/Philosophy, 7

Lisa Haverdink, MSN, Nursing, 9

Janet Heady, BSN, Nursing, 6

David Heatley, BS, Sociology/Philosophy, 8

Danny Herman, MS, Language Arts, 27

Caroline Hinton-Crenshaw, Mathematics

Michelle Hoffman, MA, Mathematics, 3

Christopher Hogan, MBA, Criminal Justice/Political Science, 3

Krystyna Hogan, MA, Language Arts, 1

Kimberly Holt, MSN, Nursing, 14

Adam Hopkins, Welding, 2

Sharon Houghton, BS, Mathematics, 7

Jeff Huff, BA, Criminal Justice, 9

Donna Hynes, RN, Nursing, 23

Ginger Imhoff, BS, Biology, 26

Peggy Imhoff, Biology, BS, 3

Riki Jensen, Business, BBA, Business, 1

Claude Johnson, BA, Criminal Justice, 2

Rachel Johansen-Wilczewksi, PhD, Sociology, 2

Ryan Jones, AAS, Communications, 2

Marija Karic, MA, Mathematics, 2

Darcia Kelley, MA, Business, 17

Ted Kluck, English, MA, 7

Mary Knapp, RN, Nursing, 15

Susan Kohloff, MA, Criminal Justice, 5

David Kohn, Computer Information Systems, 3

Dennis Koogler, Automotive, 5

Larry Koutz, MA, Mathematics, 11

Sally Koutz, Physical Education, 1

James Kusmierski, MFA, Arts, 13

Sara LaPointe, BSN, Nursing, 15

Clark Lincoln, BS, Biology, 14

Josh Lincoln, BS, Biology, 1

Brianne Lodholtz, Mathematics

Christopher Loiselle, MBA, Business, General Studies, 4

Kimberly Loomis-Hendee, MSN, Nursing, 3

Charlotte Lothian, MA, English, 6

Douglas Loweke, BA, Mathematics/Developmental Education, 25

Michelle Lucchesi, MA, Psychology, 3

Beth Markam, MSN, Nursing, 3

Valarie Marsden, BS, English, 6

Gerda Martuiak, MPA, Criminal Justice, 1

Cheryl Meyer, MA, English, 8

David Meyers, EdD, Psychology/Communications, 10

Valerie Millard, MS, Criminal Justice/Sociology, 6

Christopher Miller, JD, French, 5

Jeffrey Moeggenborg, MBA, Computer Information Systems, 2

Kevin Monroe, BA, Criminal Justice/YOP, 7

Douglas Moore, MA, Psychology, 7

Abbey Moreland, AA, American Sign Language, 1

Leslie Morford, MA, General Studies, 25

Gary Muentener, JD, Social Science, 1

Dennis Mulder, MA, Humanities, 11

Marisa Mumford, AA, American Sign Language, 2

Susan Muns, BSN, Nursing, 17

Kathleen Murray, MS, Biology, 7

David Nelson, MS, Computer Information Systems, 3

Karen Nickerson, BA, English/Spanish, 25

Victoria Olson, AA, Nursing/Allied Health, 7

Sue Ellen Pabst, MSW, Psychology, 8

Glennes Page, BS, Criminal Justice, 3

Donald Paguio, BS, Biology, 1

Lori Palmer, BS, Mathematics, 13

Edward Parish, MA, English, 6

Kenneth Parker, MA, Mathematics, 12

David Pasquale, MPA, History/Political Science, 2

Carrie Paulen, MEd, Language Arts, 2

Katey Peacock, BS, Mathematics, 2

Roberta Peacock, BSN, Nursing, 4

ShaunAnn Peters, BS, Biology, 7

Clayton Powell, Automotive, 5

Robert Powers, MA, Mathematics, 8

Todd Price, MS, Business, 8

Sheryl Pryor, BA, Business, 1

Julia Quisenberry, MA, Mathematics, 8

Mary Readwin, BSN, Nursing, 6

Douglas Reinsmith, BSN, Nursing, 10

Amie Renner, MA, Mathematics, 5

Ruth Rittersdorf, BS, General Studies, 2

Sarah Roak, MA, Language Arts, 1

Randy Robson, MA, Mathematics, 4

Diane Roose, MS, Nursing, 2

Jeannie Sage, MSN, Nursing, 3

Nancy Seals, ADN, Nursing, 12

Angela Shuart, MSN, Nursing, 1

Jill Singleton, BA, Language Arts, 1

Tore Skogseth, MA, General Studies, 6

Allen Smith, Automotive Mechanics, 7

Eric Smith, Criminal Justice, 14

Daniel Snook, MA, Developmental Education 25

Kenneth Snow, PhD, Mathematics, 24

Marjorie Sorensen, BS, Philosophy, 7

Andrea Spencer-Kelmer, BSN, Nursing, 4

Robert Spohr, MA, Business, 9

Shelly Strautz-Springborn, BA, Business/Communications, 1

Melissa Staff, BS, Allied Health, 2

Michael Stafford, PhD, Archeology, 4

Chris Stander, Physical Education, 30

Natalie Steensma, MS, Psychology, 2

Hollie Stephenson, MA, Education, 7

Connie Stewart, MBA, Business, 1

Kelsie Stoltenow, MA, Language Arts, 2

Traci Stone, MA, Early Childhood Development, 3

John Strudwick, JD, Criminal Justice, 21

Melissa Studley, BS, Computer Information Systems, 6

Krystina Stump, BA, General Studies, 4

Seth Sutton, BFA, Graphic Design, 1

Cici Broughton Sun Ting, BA, Language Arts, 1

Keith Swanson, AA, Physical Education, 2

Krystyna Sweeney, MA, Philosophy, 4

Marilynn Switzer, MSN, Nursing, 2

Melody Teegardin, MSN, Nursing, 12

Cyndee Thorlund, MSN, Nursing, 2

Kresta Train, MA, Language Arts, 3

Shannon Trip, MEd, Business, 2

Ruanne VanderVeen, RN, Nursing, 9

Philip VanDop, MDiv, Psychology, 1

Robin Wagner, PhD, Early Childhood Development, 2

Kevin Wagonmaker, MA, Computer Information Systems, 2

Martin Weese, BS, Chemistry, 2

Nicole White, BBA, Physical Education, 4

Rachel Whitmore, AA, American Sign Language, 1

Casey Carr, MS, Biology, 3

Cindy Wilson, AAS, Nursing, 10

Yonker, Patricia, BA, Mathematics/Science, 2

Adjunct Faculty Award Recipients

Outstanding Adjunct Faculty Award

2003, Barbara Day, Computer Information Systems

2004, Ginger Imhoff, Biology

2005, Lissa Sainz, General Studies

2006, Kenneth Parker, Mathematics

2007, Beverly Gates, Mathematics

2008, Debbie Bell, Visual Arts

2009, Karmen Hollis-Etter, Biology

2010, Kelly DeLong, Social Science

2011, Jeff Huff, Criminal Justice

2012, Larry Moss, English

2013, Kenneth Parker, Mathematics

2014, Lori Palmer, Mathematics

2015, Jamey Nichols, Communications/Psychology

Administrative Staff – Full Time 2015 (Name, Degree, Most Recent Position, Years)

Debra Alexander, MA, Dean of Student and Enrollment Services, 13

Angie Benn, Food Service/Subway Manager, 2

Jody Butler, BA, Creative Director, 17

Melissa Christensen, BS, Development Director, 3

Lori Cook, BS, CIS Lab Supervisor, 11

Darcella Daws, AAAS, Administrative Systems Manager, 26

Linda Devries, BS, Financial Aid Coordinator, 7

Amy Eady, MS, Dean of Health Occupations, 13

Vladimir Edelman, BS, Research Analyst, 1

Robert Ferrentino, JD, President, 6

Lisa Gardner, BBA, Student Services Coordinator, 16

George Germain, BS, Director of Facilities, 17

Jessica Gilbertson, BA, Student Success Director, 5

Terra Guild, BA, Director of MCC's Barnes & Noble Bookstore, 1

Susan Hatto, MA, Dean of Community and Workforce Ed., 9

Gary Hauck, PhD, Dean of Instr. and Student Development, 7

Jessica Herrick, BA, Assistant Director of Financial Aid, 5

David Kohn, BS, Assistant Director of Information Technology, 3

Lisa Lund, MS, Director of Institutional Effectiveness, 4

Rod Middleton, AAAS, Director of IT, 31

Traci Nichols, BA, Dir. of Financial Aid, 9

Doug Reinsmith, BSN, Nursing Lab Coordinator, 7

Therese Smith, MA, Exec. Dir. Of MCC Foundation/Assistant to the President, 28

Robert Spohr, MS, VP for Student and Academic Affairs, 12

Shelly Strautz-Springborn, BS, Communications Director, 8

Connie Stewart, MA, Director of Human Resources, 5

Delores Thompson, BS, Staff Accountant, 15

Kire Wierda, BS, Director of Accounting, 3

Ryan Wilson, BS, Director of Student and Community Outreach, 3

Administrative Staff – Full Time 2015 Profiles

Debra Alexander is an MCC and CMU grad. She has an associate degree in applied arts and sciences, business administration and an associate in arts and sciences from MCC; and from CMU a bachelor of science in business administration, as well as a master of arts in interpersonal and public communication. Alexander joined the MCC team in 2001 as the development officer for the MCC Foundation, then in 2004 became the director of admissions. In 2010 she was promoted to associate dean of student services, and in 2012 was selected for the position of dean of student and enrollment services at MCC. She previously was part-owner of Oakley Hardwoods, a hardwood lumber mill, and the Gratiot Branch Manager of Mid-Michigan Industries

Angie Benn is MCC's Subway Manager and Food Service Director. She joined MCC in January 2014. Before MCC, she was a Subway Field Consultant. Benn has a manager course of study diploma and is food safety certified.

Melissa Christensen is the development director for MCC. She has worked in the non-profit arena for more than 10 years getting her start as a Michigan Main Street manager for the community of Portland. She has a BA in marketing from the University of Phoenix and is pursuing her MA in management and leadership. In addition to organizing employee socials, fundraising functions, alumni relations and development projects she also teaches a college success course at MCC.

Linda DeVries began working at MCC in August 2006 as the accounts receivable/billing coordinator and in January 2013 began working as the financial aid coordinator. She has an AA from Davenport College in accounting/computer information systems and a BS in accounting from Davenport University. Prior to coming to MCC, DeVries worked in manufacturing accounting for 10 years, was a stay at home mom for about six years, worked at GRCC for two years and worked as a bookkeeper and office manager at a church.

Amy Eady became a full-time faculty member in 2004 after serving as an adjunct instructor at MCC, and was appointed dean of health occupations in 2013. She holds a BS in medical technology & biology from Saginaw Valley State University, and an MS (CTE) from Ferris State University. Her credentials also include MT(ASCP) and RMA(AMT).

Eady has taught several courses in allied health and guest lectures in the department of nursing.

Lisa Gardner began her time at MCC as a student in 1997. In the fall of 1998, she began a part-time lab assistant position in the Computer Information Systems Lab. Later in 2002, Gardner advanced to a full-time position in the student success and testing center and in 2011 to her current position of student development coordinator and academic advisor. She earned her AA degree from MCC, then transferred and completed her BBA at Northwood University. She is currently working toward her MA in career and technical education at Ferris State University. In addition to academic advising, Gardner works closely with students in a variety of projects related to student success and completion, such as academic referral, career connections, student clubs and activities, and new student orientation. She is also a strong proponent of lifelong learning.

George Germain has been the director of facilities at MCC since August 1998. He has a BS in business administration with a marketing major from Central Michigan University. During Germain's tenure, the college has added a second campus in Greenville and added some 114,000 square feet of space. The college also built its first two LEED buildings: The Stanley P. Ash Building in Sidney and the Bill Braman Family Center for Education in Greenville.

Germain has also served as a member of the adjunct faculty teaching courses in algebra, marketing, management, advertising, and right triangle trigonometry. He is a lifelong resident of Montcalm County and currently resides in the Stanton area.

Jessica Gilbertson has been the student success director since 2010. She earned her associate of liberal studies from MCC and her BA in communications and education from Aquinas College. She has teaching experience as an adjunct instructor in college success, biology, and communications. Her certifications are in secondary education (state of Michigan) and as a supplemental instruction trainer/supervisor through

University of Kansas City in Missouri. Gilbertson has extensive experience serving and assisting students through her multiple professional roles as supplemental instruction program coordinator, online and face-to-face tutoring coordinator, campus testing coordinator, student success help desk coordinator, and a Veterans Club advisor. Gilbertson served in the United States Army as broadcast journalist and public affairs specialist in support of both Operation Enduring Freedom and Operation Iraqi Freedom. She is a 20-year member of the Flat River Community Players and the head costumer for the Flat River Dance Company.

Jessica Herrick is MCC's assistant director of financial aid. She joined the college in November 2010. She disburses federal, state and institutional aid for MCC students; coordinates the federal campus work study contracts; awards and monitors the Michigan Competitive Program; and coordinates the State of Michigan Tuition Incentive Program (TIP) with the State of Michigan and the MCC Business Office. Prior to MCC, she worked at Davenport University as a financial aid coordinator. Herrick earned an associate degree in management in 2002 and bachelor's degree in management in 2009, both from Davenport University.

Ginger Imhoff joined the college in 1988 as the science lab supervisor. Before MCC, she was a stay-at-home mom. She then came to MCC in 1987 to "find herself" and started working part-time in 1988 with mentors Ken Smith and Don Stearns. After transferring to Central Michigan University and finally Ferris State University, she completed her BS in biology education in 1991. Upon graduation, Imhoff was hired full-time as the science lab supervisor. Over the course of her years at MCC, she has also taught anatomy & physiology online, botany and biology, while directing the instructional science labs' operations and training lab personnel.

Lisa Lund earned a BS in family community services with honors from Michigan State University in 1991. Three years later in 1994, she earned a master of social work degree with a policy, planning, and administration emphasis from Western Michigan University. She is a licensed social worker in Michigan.

Since 2011, Lund has served as director of institutional effectiveness at MCC. Key responsibilities of that position include AQIP accreditation pathway activity coordination, grant writing, institutional reporting, institutional research, and assessment.

For 17 years prior to coming to MCC, she served as coordinator for the Montcalm Human Services Coalition. In that role, she provided leadership for a group of more than 30 organizations working collaboratively to address a wide range of community needs within Montcalm County.

As a resident of Montcalm County for 20 years, her community involvement includes leadership positions on groups including the Greenville Area and Michigan Jaycees, Leadership Montcalm, United Way of Montcalm County, Central Montcalm Community Foundation, Montcalm County Planning Commission, and the Central Montcalm Elementary PTO. Two of her most cherished honors were being selected as a fellow in the Michigan Political Leadership Program (2000) and being recognized as the Women's Action Network's Woman of the Year in 2005. In 2014, she will complete a three-year term of service as membership coordinator for the Michigan Association for Institutional Research Steering Committee.

Rod Middleton studied at MCC before going to Lansing Community College and Davenport University. Middleton has worked at MCC in the technology department since 1984 as a programmer and sole employee helping to implement the first computerized registration system. In the 30 years since that time he has helped build the information technology services department, which has connected the college campuses and connected to the Internet and implemented the first website, email and online services. Rod enjoys mountain biking, gardening, history and making beer.

Traci Nichols is MCC's director of financial aid. Between 1993 and 1998, she was a financial aid work study and financial aid clerk. She returned to MCC in July 2006 as the assistant director of financial aid and became the director in 2010. Her duties include ensuring compliance of awarding, disbursing and reporting of federal, state and institutional student financial aid. Before MCC, she was a waitress and restaurant owner. Nichols earned associate degrees in accounting and business data processing from MCC and a BS in business administration from Franklin University.

Terry Smith came to MCC in March 1987. She has served the college in several advancement capacities as assistant to the president, board of trustees assistant secretary, public information director, director of institutional advancement, vice president for institutional advancement and foundation executive director. Smith attended Lansing Community College, then earned her BA degree in journalism from Michigan State University and her MA degree in community college leadership from Antioch University McGregor. She also completed coursework toward her certificate in fundraising management in The Fund Raising School at the Indiana University Lilly Family School of Philanthropy. Prior to her employment at MCC, Smith was an assistant account executive at Manning, Selvage & Lee Public Relations.

Rob Spohr came to MCC as an adjunct instructor in fall 2003, and joined the full-time faculty in fall 2005. He became dean of occupational education in 2008, and in 2009 health occupations were added to his position. In 2010, Spohr became the vice president of academic affairs, and in 2013 vice president of student and academic affairs. Spohr holds an AAS in business from MCC, a BA in marketing from Grand Valley State University, an MS in career and technical education from Ferris State University, and is a PhD candidate in higher, adult and lifelong education at Michigan State University. Prior to coming to MCC, Spohr was an electronics tech and marksmanship instructor in the United States Marine Corps, owned and operated a Domino's Pizza shop, was a production and shipping supervisor for Thornapple Valley Meats, shift superintendent/cold drink manager for the State of Michigan Dr. Pepper/7-Up, shift superintendent at Leon Plastics, and project manager and estimator for Central Ceiling & Partition.

Shelly Strautz-Springborn is MCC's communications director. She joined the college in August 2006 and has more than 20 years of experience in the communications industry. She is responsible for the college's media presence, serving as the college's primary media contact; writes and edits college publications, news releases, newsletters, brochures, direct mail pieces and other promotional materials; manages and oversees content of the college website; develops and implements the college's social networking activities; and supports the college's marketing activities. Springborn earned a bachelor's degree in agriculture and natural resources communications from Michigan State University in 1994.

Connie Stewart came to MCC in early 2011 to fill the position of director of human resources. Prior to MCC she worked in human resources at Hitachi Magnetics Corp and Morbark, Inc. She earned an AA in business from MCC, a BA in organizational management from Spring Arbor University, and an MBA from Western Governors University. She has been an active member of the Mid-Michigan Human Resource Association, Business and Professional Women's Club of Alma, Mich., and has served as treasurer of Hitachi Credit Union, treasurer of the band boosters of Montabella Community Schools and Cub Master of the Edmore Boy Scout Troop #3078.

Dolores Thompson (BS in business administration and accounting, Northern Michigan University), has served on MCC's staff since June of 2000 as staff accountant for the business office.

Administrative Staff – Part Time 2015
(Name, Degree, Most Recent Position, Years)

Katie Arwood, Library Director, 5

Ryan Kieffer, BS, Sciences Lab Supervisor, 1

Donald Burns, PhD, President Emeritus, 38

James Lantz, MBA, VP of Admin. Services, 27

Denise Edwards, BS, Director of Student Support Services, 28

Administrative Staff – Part Time 2015 Profiles

Katie Arwood is the library director at MCC. She came to MCC in August 2012. She manages MCC library materials and resources. She also promotes library services to MCC students and faculty, and to the community. Before joining MCC, she was the director for the White Pine District Library for 15 years and an outreach librarian for six years. Arwood earned a BS from Michigan State University and a master of library science degree from Wayne State University.

Jim Lantz earned his BBA with honors in accountancy from Western Michigan University. Following a year in the MBA program at the University of Michigan, he joined the certified public accounting firm of Young, Skutt & Breitenwischer (YSB) and received his CPA license. He was selected to open the firm's west Michigan office, initially located in Greenville and later relocated to Grand Rapids. In 1985, YSB merged with the statewide firm of Rehmann Robson.

In 1986, Lantz became director of business and finance at MCC, a position which grew into vice president for administrative services. This position includes responsibility for all accounting, data processing, financial aid, physical plant, human resources, purchasing, bookstore, cafeteria, risk management and budgeting activities of the College.

Lantz was honored by the national Community College Business Officers association (CCBO) in 1997 as the Outstanding Chief Business Officer of the year (region X – Michigan, Indiana, Ohio). In 2005 he was elected president of CCBO, and was re-elected to that post in 2006. He recently (2012 – 2014) served as chair of the National Association of College & University Business Officers (NACUBO) Community Colleges Council and is currently chair of the Michigan Community College Risk Management Authority. He is a past president of the Michigan Community College Business Officers Association and has presented workshops at numerous national conferences.

Lantz's community involvement includes over 30 years as a member of Rotary International, serving two terms each as president of Greenville's Danish Festival, president of Big Brothers/Big Sisters of Montcalm & Ionia Counties, and president of his church council.

Former Administrative Staff
(Name, Degree, Recent Position, Years)

Hilmer Anderson, BS, Director of Business and Finance, 4

Jean Bailey, MA, Dean of Acad. Serv., 6

Jill Baker-George, MA, Admissions Rep., 1

Wilma Baldwin, BS, Office Education Lab Supervisor, 3

Clifford, Bedore, Jr, EdD, Admin. Asst., President, 11

Howard Benson, MA, Director of Comm. Services, 7

Marsha Budd, BS, Aquatics Supervisor, 6

Janet Campbell-Shy, BS, Bookstore Director, 11

John Carlson, AMLS, Director of Learning Resources Center, 24

Amyee Carson, MSW, Director of Community Outreach, 4

Lisa Castro, AAAS, Food Service/Subway Manager, 1

Richard Conrath, PhD, VP for Instruction, 3

Holly Cook, BS, Director of Community Services, 11

Verla Cummings, BA, Librarian, 4

Kendall Downing, MA, Director of COPE, 2

Eron Drake, MA, Dean of Inst. and Comm. Serv., 4

Catherine Earl, MSN., PhD, Dean of Nursing and Allied Health, 10

Jane Faussett, Skills Development Lab Supervisor, 7

Elizabeth Felts, BA, Director of Institutional Advancement, 2

Donald Fink, EdD, President, 5

Susan Fizer, BA, YOP Director, 4

Charlotte Fokens, PhD, Special Needs Supervisor, 3

Margery Forist, BS, Director of Accounting, 26

Jesse Fox, MA, Director of Technical Studies, 5

Walter Frick, AAS, Food Service Director, 2

Brian Gardner, BS, Development Officer, 4

Robert Gravelle, MA, Dean of Academic Studies, 4

Jenny Griffiths, MSN, Dean of Nursing and Allied Health, 2

Roger Hale, MS, Director of Financial Aid, 4

Connie Haling, Financial Aid Officer, 8

Richard Heckman, EdD, Vice President for Instruction, 4

Danny Herman, MA, Dean of Occ. Prog., 23

Beverly Hilscher, BS, RN, Director of Business and Industry Development, 2

Barbara Hofmeister-Carter, MS, RN, Dir. of Nursing Education and Allied Health, 4

Lon Holton, MA, Dean of Student Services, 22

Jeff Huff, BS, Youthful Offender Program Recruiter, 2

Ginger Imhoff, Nat. Science Lab Supervisor, 20

James Kirk, MA, Dean of Students, 4

Charles Krug, MS, Vice President for Instruction, 2

Carol Krumbach, BS, Director of Admissions, 5

Stephen Lindeman, MA, Youthful Offender Project Supervisor, 2

James Lucka, MA, Counselor, 36

Gary Lund, MEd, Dean of Technical Studies, 5

Phil, Lund, Jr, JD, Director of Business and Industry Development, 4

William Lymangrover, EdS, Director of Community Services, 3

Sally Mathisen, AAS, Registrar, 10

Keith Miller, PhD, VP for Inst. Ser., 6

Robert Minnick, Registrar, 3

Gary Moore, MA, Dean of Vocational/Technical Studies, 2

Sally Morais, BS, Director of Enrollment Services, 10

Leslie Morford, MA, Dean of Academic Studies, 4

Gloria Morrison, MA, Counselor, 3

Dennis Mulder, MA, Dean of Liberal Arts, 23

Donald Mullins, MA, Counselor, 3

Susan Muns, BSN, Health Occupations Lab Supervisor, 2

Denise Newman, PhD, Dean of Student Services, 2

Kathleen Olsen-Lofts, BA, Dean of Students, 16

Donald Olson, MA, Dean of Vocational/Technical Studies, 6

Richard Parker, MLS, Director of Library, 20

Gordon Peltier, Business Manager, 7

Alden Perkins, AA, Bursar, 15

Jill Pickens, Bookstore Director

Rebecca Powell, BA, Director of Financial Aid, 16

David Pilon, MA, Director of Occupational Education, 1

Frank Reeder, Maintenance Superintendent, 21

Jo Ann Regis, BS, Director of Practical Nursing, 12

Gregg Robinson, AAAS, Food Service Director, 9

Lisa Rosier, AS, Food Service/ Subway Manager, 1

Angie Sattler, MA, Student Services Coordinator/Advisor, 1

Joseph Skupin, MA, Director of Occupational Education, 1

Kenneth Snow, PhD, Vice President for Instruction, 6

Lois Springsteen, Director of Public Information, 13

Donald Stearns, MA, Activities Planning Director, 2

Herbert Stoutenburg, EdD, President, 6

Maria Suchowski, PhD, Director of Assessment of Institutional Research, 9

Maurice Swift, MA, Dean of Vocational/Technical Studies, 3

William Tammone, PhD, VP for Academic Services, 12

Marvel Teunisson, BS, Technology Support Coordinator, 14

Charles Tetzlaff, BS, Librarian, 4

Maribeth Tronsen, BS, Director of Consumer Education, 2

Robert Tupper, EdS, Dean of Students, 4

Michael Turnbull, MA, Director of Admissions and Financial Aid, 3

Susan Wambach, RN, MSN, Associate Dean of Health Occupations, 6

Helen Whitmer, BSEd, Skills Development Lab Supervisor, 14

Patricia Willison, Director of Continuing Education, 12

Leslie Wood, MA, Director of Workforce Training Solutions, 11

Leadership Award Recipients

MCC Leadership Award

2002, Kathleen Lofts, Director of Enrollment Services

2003, Patricia Willison, Director of Continuing Education

2004, Margery Forist, Director of Accounting

2005, Debra Alexander, Director of Admissions

2006, Denise Edwards, Director of Enrollment Services

2007, Therese Smith, Public Information System Director/ Assistant to the President

2008, Rodney Middleton, Information Systems Director

2009, Robert Spohr, Dean of Occupational Education

2010, Jody Hedrick, Publications Coordinator/Graphic Designer

2011, Gary Hauck, Dean of Instruction and Faculty

2012, Marvel Teunissen, Technology Support Coordinator

2013, Susan Hatto, Dean of Community and Workforce Education

2014, David Kohn, Assistant Director of Information Technology

2015, Connie Stewart, Director of Human Resources

Support Staff – Full Time 2015
(Name, Degree, Recent Position, Years)

Michelle Adams, BSB, Custodian, 9

Karen Buskirk, Food Services Assistant/Subway, 15

Joseph Codling, BBS, Student Success Administrative Assistant, 3

Kevin Evoy, Maintenance, 25

Heather Fierke, BS, Health Occupations Administrative Assistant, 11

Angela Frye, BBA, Financial Aid Advisor, 1

Randall Gilbert, AAAS, IT Specialist, 14

Pam Grice, Student Services Support Specialist, 23

Ann Hansen, Custodian, 27

Sheila Hansen, AAAS, Accounts Receivable/Billing Coordinator, 5

Tammy Headworth, AAS, Institutional Effectiveness Assistant, 25

Lisa Herald, Executive Assistant to the President's Office, 10

Serena Houseman, AAS, Administrative Assistant for Academic Affairs, 15

Michael Jaworowicz, Maintenance, 2

Virgil Jurden, Custodian, 9

Breanna Lintemuth, AGS, Digital Services Coordinator, 2

Dawn Lyke, AAAS, Payroll Manager, 15

Mary Jo McCully, AAAS, Student and Academic Affairs Administrative Assistant, 11

Rodney Nutt, IT Specialist, 30

Phyllis Pollock, Custodian, 15

Doreen Richmond, AAS, Financial Aid Advisor, 9

Mark Ryan, Maintenance, 25

Billie Sanders, AAS, Custodian, 5

Gary Shilling, Custodian, 14

Jeniffer Smith, AGS, Assistant Manager of MCC's Barnes & Noble Bookstore, 6

Christine Stander, Recreation Program Coordinator, 30

Julie Stockwell, Administrative Services Assistant, 25

Ann Wiggers, AAS, Accounting Assistant, 11

Glenda Stoudt, Custodian, 18

Marquitta Stubblefield, BA, Custodian, 13

Amberlea Zimmerman, BAS, Student and Enrollment Services Specialist, 6

Support Staff – Full Time 2015 Profiles

Karen Buskirk is a food service assistant at MCC. She joined the college in August 2000. She ensures that Subway is running smoothly while keeping up with the changes within the restaurant chain. Before MCC, she worked at Carson City Hospital. Buskirk has a national certification in food safety.

Randall Gilbert is the information technology specialist at MCC. He joined the college in 2001. He supports and monitors application software systems; installs, maintains, documents and troubleshoots the network, while maintaining its inventory; and assists the staff concerning any problems with the campus-wide technology. Before MCC, he was a construction worker.

Pam Grice is MCC's student services support specialist. She joined the college in April 1992. Her primary duties are admissions, registration and new student contact. She also serves as a support for the dean of student and enrollment services and director of recruitment, enrollment & outreach. Before MCC, she worked in food service and restaurant management. Grice earned an associate of general studies from MCC in 1999.

Sheila Hansen is an accounts receivable and billing coordinator at MCC. She came to MCC in August 2010. Her main duties include creating invoices, processing student and vendor payments, answering questions about student accounts and serving as a backup for Admissions. Before MCC, she worked in accounting for almost 30 years without a degree. She last worked in Lowell for a furniture manufacturer, serving as their accountant while also taking on many other tasks. Hansen earned an associate degree in accounting from MCC in 2011.

Tammy Headworth is MCC's institutional effectiveness assistant. She joined the college in 1990. Her primary duties are pulling and submitting information for state and federal reports, as well as setting up queries for reports and surveys. Before MCC, she worked at Foremost Insurance Company. Headworth earned an associate of applied science from Davenport College in 1986.

Lisa Herald is the executive assistant for the president's office. She started at MCC as an admissions work study in 2005, working her way to two different part-time positions before becoming full-time in 2008 and adding her current duties in 2012. She provides high-level administrative support to the executive director of the MCC Foundation, president and MCC Board of Trustees. Before MCC, she worked for Meijer for 10 years and was a stay-at-home mom. Herald is currently working toward her associate of applied science in office administration at MCC.

Anne Wiggers is an accounting assistant in MCC's business office. She joined MCC full time in 2004. She manages accounts payable, bank deposits and account reconciliations. Before MCC, she raised her family while giving music lessons and working part-time as a bank teller and accounts payable representative. Wiggers earned an AAS from MCC in 2004 and a bachelor's degree in human resources from Franklin University in 2009.

Support Staff – Part Time 2015
(Name, Degree, Recent Position, Years)

Emily Ackerson, SIL Monitor, 1

Ashley Allerding, SIL Monitor

Dana Alexander-Brom, SIL Tutor, Lab Monitor, and Lab Assistant

Harmony Battreall, BA, Human Resources Assistant, 2

Michelle Becker, BBA, Lab Assistant, 1

Caron Bianchi, Student Services Support Assistant, 2

Terri Burns, Lab Supervisor, 1

Emily Carmey, ALS, SIL Lab Supervisor, 1

Jillian Chapko, Recreation Desk Monitor, 1

Randi Claybaugh, Lifeguard, 1

Tiffany Claybaugh, Recreation Desk Monitor and Lifeguard, 1

Katelyn Clementz, AAS, Student Services Assistant, 1

Ethan Coe, Recreation Desk Monitor, 1

Dana Cunningham, AAS, Lab Assistant, 27

Jacob deFluiter, Lab Assistant, 1

Laura Delamater, SIL Monitor, 1

Eliana Drake, Lifeguard, 1

Joseph Dunn, Student Tutor

Heather Eastman, Lifeguard, 10

Andrea Edelman, BS, Lab Supervisor, 2

Elizabeth Enos, SIL Monitor, 2

Erin Ferguson, Recreation Desk Monitor, 1

Gregory Gardner, BS, Supplemental Instructional Leader, 6

Nicholas Gorney, BBM, Service Desk Tech and Lab Assistant, 3

Sara Hansen, BA, Supplemental Instructional Leader, 1

Hanna Harrington, Lab Assistant, 1

Johnathon Heath, ALS, Lab Assistant, 4

Sarin Hoogeveen, AA, Lab Assistant, 2

Amber Jaramillo, BS, Professional Tutor and Lab Supervisor, 9

Lisa Johnson, BA, Library Assistant, 9

Jennifer Jones, Student Tutor

Barbara Kaaikala, Lab Assistant, 2

Morgan Kamp, SIL Monitor, 1

Haylee Kimball, SIL Monitor

Kevin Knowlton, Lab Monitor, 1

Nancy Knowlton, BS, Lab Assistant, 9

Patricia Kooi, MA, Lab Monitor, 1

Anthony Kosal, AAS, Service Desk Tech and Lab Assistant, 2

Joseph Lake, Lab Assistant, 2

Betty-Jane Leeuw, AAS, Lab Assistant, 4

Heather Leonard, BBA, Recreation Desk Monitor, 1

Meagan Lintemuth, Student Tutor

Samantha Mack, BA, Writer, 2

Caleb Marvin, Lifeguard, 2

Karen Maxfield, BA, Cultural Events Coordinator, 2

Sasha Michalek, RN, Professional Tutor, 1

Susan Moss, BA, Instructional Services Assistant, 5

Ellen Nelson, SIL Monitor, 1

Jeffrey Nolan, BS, Professional Tutor, 1

Corey Osborne, SIL Monitor, 1

Shirley Palmer, Lab Assistant, 12

Donald Pellow, Lab Assistant, 2

Diego Pignanessi, Lifeguard, 1

Jerry Poprawski, BS, Lab Monitor, 15

Kori Post, SIL Monitor, 1

Roxie Poulsen, AAS, Lab Assistant, 8

Anthony Raymor, SIL Monitor, 1

Peter Reno, BSBA, Lab Assistant, 1

Heather Rogers, AA, Recreation Desk Monitor, 3

Timothy Rogers, AAS, Lab Supervisor, 6

Saydee Rowland, SIL Monitor, 1

Michael Ruggles, Lab Assistant, 1

Peter Saladin, SIL Monitor, 1

Kelsey Shattuck, AA, Graphic Design Assistant, 1

Danielle Smith, BS, Professional Tutor, 1

Brandie Spencer, SIL Monitor, 1

Ryan Syrek, Lab Monitor, 1

Amy Throop, BSBA, Library Assistant, 1

Kaleigh Vanderlip, Student Tutor

Shawn VanNortrick, BA, Service Desk Technician and Lab Assistant, 2

Lois Westfall, AA, Lab Assistant, 1

John White, AAS, Lab Monitor, 1

Kaitlyn Wietsma, SIL Monitor

Eric Wisniewski, BS, Professional Tutor, 2

Christine Yoder, Instructional Services Assistant, 8

Support Staff – Part Time 2015 Profiles

Lisa Johnson is a library assistant at MCC. She joined the college out of high school in September 1996 as a student tutor. She has also been a professional tutor and business communications adjunct instructor. She has worked various jobs including working at a hardware store and assisting author Gary Eberle with book research. Currently, she assists students with library databases and reference questions. She also assists in all library operations, including new book processing. Johnson earned a BA in English from Aquinas College in 2006.

Samantha Mack is MCC's Part-time Communications Assistant. She joined MCC in February 2014. She assists Communications Director Shelly Strautz-Springborn with writing news releases, "Happenings," "Keeping Posted," alumni stories and feature stories for *Career Focus*. She also edits *Career Focus* and *Life Focus*, and takes photographs for various projects. In addition, she works at *The Rockford Squire* newspaper in Rockford as an administrative assistant and freelance writer. Mack earned a BA in writing from Bluffton University in Bluffton, Ohio, in August 2013. She also minored in music and peace and conflict studies.

Karen Maxfield first entered the MCC family as a work study for the human resources department in 2008 under Anne McCoy. She then transferred to Alma College in 2010, where she earned her BA in philosophy in 2012. Longing to return to MCC, she was hired part-time as a cultural events coordinator in 2013, and also took on a part-time position updating web pages for the communications department in 2014. Maxfield is an accomplished musician and is a member of several local, performing ensembles.

Susan Moss works in instructional services and is an administrative assistant on MCC's Greenville campus. She joined the college in August 2010. Her main duties include working with continuing education and noncredit classes, data entry, communicating with students and instructors concerning class updates, proctoring tests, managing the reception desk and security at the Ash TLC and the Braman Center. She has been the secretary for the First Congregational Church of Greenville for 18 years. Moss earned a BA from Northern Illinois University in 2000.

Kelsey Shattuck is the part-time graphic design assistant at MCC. She joined the college in April 2014. She assists Creative Director Jody Butler with designing newsletters, event flyers, posters and brochures; formatting layout for many of the college's publications and promotional materials; and taking photographs of the college's buildings and events. Shattuck is currently studying graphic design at Lansing Community College and plans to transfer to Kendall College of Art and Design in fall 2015.

Christine Yoder is a part-time instructional services assistant on MCC's Greenville campus. She started as a work study in 2005. In 2007, she worked at the Harold O. Steele Education Center in Fenwick. In 2010, she returned to MCC as an administrative assistant at the Ash TLC. She has also been a librarian assistant at the White Pine District Library since 2005. Yoder earned a theological certificate from Kentucky Mountain Bible College as well as an associate of general studies and an associate of applied science from MCC.

Former Support Staff – Full Time

Cora Arutoff-Heaton, AA, 3

Hope Badge, 14

Jean Barker

Jon Brand, 35

Janet Campbell, BBA, 21

Judy Castro, BA, 5

John Christiansen, 35

Gaylerd Cooper, 18

Carolyn Corwin

Joseph Edwards, BBA, 9

Eugene Ehle, 35

Michelle Ehlert-Peckham, AAS, 12

Jeanne Falzon, BRE, 12

William Gall, Jr., 10

Darcie Goodenough-Lopez, AAS, 2

Susan Greene, 2

Mark Guyette, BS, 4

Laurie Harris-Lackey, 8

Tammy Headworth, AA, 25

Lori Holland, 1

Carol Hopkins, 22

Shirley Inbody, 10

Julie Kavanagh

Vada Keyes, 13

Jane LaLonde, AAAS, 33

Rebecca Lewis

Mary Ellen Lingeman, 29

Nikki Lopez, AA, 1

Juanita Mertens, AGS, 7

Sharon Minnick, AAS, 17

Norman Moon, BBA, 24

Michelle Moreland Becker, 5

Hope Newburg, AS, 12

Tracy Pike, 2

Patricia Reeder, AS, 8

Kristina Reinsmith, 3

Joseph Rose, BS, 5

Tina Ruid, 4

Nicole Santino, 2

Bonnie Schlosser

Heidi Schumacher-Fare, AA, 1

Patricia Seaver, 1

Jonathan Sheathelm

Kelly Sigler, 3

Jeniffer Smith, AAAS, 6

Tracy Snider, 3

Judith Snyder, 21

Mathew Soper, 3

Karen Stevens, AA, 42

Sharon Thomasson, BRE, 1

George Thompson, MA, 3

Marilyn Thomsen, 20

Ly Sing Ung, 5

Alma Urie, 16

Barbara Warschefsky, BS, 14

Michelle Webber-Mazerkewicz, AAAS, 9

Anne White, 3

Staff Award Recipients

Alden Perkins Dedicated Service Award

1986, Leo Wheeler

1987, Jane LaLonde

1988, Patricia Willison

1989, Karen Stevens

1990, Sharon Minnick

1991, Kathleen Olsen

1992, Alma Urie

1993, Mary Ellen Lingeman

1994, Carolyn Corwin

1995, Kenneth Brygal

1996, Marilyn Thomsen

1997, John, Sr. Christiansen

1998, Darcella Daws

1999, Mark Ryan

2000, Norman Moon

2001, Barbara Warschefsky

2002, Glenda Stoudt

2003, Lisa Gardner

2004, Randall Gilbert

2005, Karen Buskirk

2006, Amberlea Zimmerman

2007, Joe Brand

2008, Christine Stander

2009, Julie Stockwell

2010, Kevin Evoy

2011, Ann Hansen

2012, Pam Grice

2013, Mary Jo McCully

2014, Rodney Nutt

Distinguished Service Award Recipients

MCC Stanley & Blanche Ash Distinguished Service Award

1973, Stanley Ash

1973, Dr. W. Bruce Bennett

1973, Joseph Cook

1973, James Crosby

1973, L. Stanley Kemp

1973, Marian Kemp

1973, Kenneth Lehman

1973, Dr. William Seiter

1974, Dr. Harold Steele

1974, Maurice Swift

1975, Grace Greenhoe

1975, Bill Braman

1976, Dr. Larry Disher

1977, Dr. Ahmad Younis

1978, Michael Slentz

1979, Michael Salisbury

1979, Dr. Arthur Kurtze

1980, Margery Wilson

1980, Stanton Development

1980, Lester J. Sitts VFW Post 5065

1981, Harold Springsteen

1981, Einer Thorlund, Jr.

1982, Francis Rivard

1983, Sydney Swainston

1983, Vernon Johnson

1984, Donald McKenna

1985, Robert Welborn

1985, Donald Van Singel

1986, Paul Warnshuis

1986, David Mayes

1987, George Showers

1987, Gordon Stauffer

1988, John Stafford & *The Daily News*

1988, Eric Halvorsen

1989, C. Homer Miel

1989, Women's Festival Council

1990, L. Charles Mulholland

1990, Montcalm Heritage Village Committee

1991, Wayne Omillian

1991, Edmore Woman's Club

1993, Orville Trebian

1993, Robert Braman

1994, Robert Marston

1995, David Camp

1995, David Roslund

1996, Panhandle Coalition

1996, Coalition of Greater Greenville

1997, Montcalm Alliance

1997, Joanne Emmons

1998, Beatrice Doser

1998, EightCAP, Inc.

1999, Lemont Renterghem

2000, Larry DeVuyst

2000, Judith Riessen

2000, Charles Halterman

2001, M-TEC Campaign Leadership Team

2002, M-TEC Board of Overseers

2003, Thomas Kohn

2003, Jean Southward

2004, Franz Mogdis

2004, Robert Painter

2005, Judy Emmons

2005, Alan Cropsey

2006, Central Area Michigan Works! Consortium

2008, Blanche Ash

2009, United Solar Ovonic

2010, Steve Foster

2011, William & Harriette Cook

2012, Richard Ellafrits

2013, Martha Jean Brundage

2014, Creating Futures, Strengthening Partnerships Campaign Team

2015, Leslie Morford

Top tier: Social Science Instructor Michael Seaman, Mathematics Instructor Jan Roy; Middle tier: Performing Arts Coordinator Valerie Vander Mark, Visual Arts Coordinator Carolyn Johnson; Lower tier: Vice President for Student and Academic Affairs Rob Spohr, Dean of Community and Workforce Education Susan Hatto

Top tier: Retired MCC staff members and instructors met in October 2014. Middle tier: Earlier photos of retired Director of Enrollment Services Denise Edwards and retired Language Arts Instructor Jim Fatka; Bottom tier: Earlier photos of retired Vice President for Administrative Services James Lantz and Student Services Support Specialist Karen Stevens.

Sources

Ameling, Kelli. "MCC Greenville Building to be Named after the Braman Family." *The Daily News* [Greenville, MI] 5 Apr. 2013. Print.

Beard, Kathleen. Letter to the author. 8 Feb. 2011. Handwritten.

Braman, Bill. Personal interview. 1 Jul. 2014.

Brundage, Jean. Personal interview. 12 Nov. 2010.

Burch, Chip. "A Sporting School." *The Daily News* [Greenville, MI] 30 Dec. 2005. Print.

Burns, Donald. Letter to Paul Martin. 14 Oct. 1986. Typescript.

Burns, Donald. Meeting conversation. 12 Jan. 2015.

Burns, Donald. Personal conversation. 30 May 2013.

Burns, Donald. Personal interview. 23 Jul. 2012.

Burns, Donald. Personal interview regarding Heritage Village. 9 Feb. 2011.

Butler, Jody. Personal interview. 28 Jul. 2014.

Carbonelli, Karen. Personal interview. 1 Jul. 2014.

Carpenter, Judy, Grant Elliot, and Candy Jorgenson. *MCC Time Capsule*. Rec. 26 Apr. 1976. Montcalm Community College, 1976. Cassette.

Christensen, Linda. "Area Couple Celebrate 75 Years of Marital Bliss," *The Daily News* [Greenville, MI] 16 Jan. 1997. Sec. 1:6+. Print.

Christophersen, Lillian. Letter to the author. 5 Mar. 2011. Handwritten.

Cole, Nate. "From Jail Cells to Computer Labs." *The Daily News* [Greenville, MI] 27 Dec. 2005. Print.

Conaway, John. "Clifford Bedore Hired by Community College." *The Daily News* [Greenville, MI] 2 Jul. 1965. Print.

Cummings, Verla. Letter to Terry Smith. 24 May 2004. Email.

DeLong, Kenric. Personal interview. 23 May 2014.

Edwards, Denise. Letter to author. 21 Oct. 2013. Email.

Ferrentino, Robert. Personal interview. 6 Jun. 2014.

Ferrentino, Bob. *Strategic Plan for 2010-2012.* Sidney, MI: Montcalm Community College, 2010. Print.

Fox, Jesse. Letter to the author. 16 Feb. 2011. Handwritten.

Fox, Jesse. Personal interview. 6 Jun. 2014.

Fox, Jesse. Telephone interview regarding Heritage Village. 11 Apr. 2011.

Gates, Beverly. Personal interview. 30 Jul. 2014.

Grand Rapids Press. "Mrs. Manfred Doser Named Publicity Chairman." [Grand Rapids, MI] 29 Oct. 1964. Print.

Grand Rapids Press. "Jerry Freid is Dead, A Victim of the Neighborhood He Loved [Grand Rapids, MI] 26 Apr. 1977. Print.

Harris, Maxine. Letter to the author. 1 Mar. 2011. Handwritten.

Hauck, Gary. *The Story of Heritage Village – Celebrating 25 Years.* Bloomington, IN: iUniverse, Inc., 2011. Print.

Heritage Village. *Constitution of the Heritage Village Committee, Inc.* Sidney, MI: Montcalm Community College, n.d. Print.

Heritage Village. *School Days*. Sidney, MI: Montcalm Community College, 1987. Print.

Horvath, Rosemary. "Burns Still Enthusiastic about MCC's Direction." *The Daily News* [Greenville, MI] 2 Aug. 1999. Print.

Horvath, Rosemary. "Community Breaks Ground on New Center." *The Daily News* [Greenville, MI] 17 Jun. 1999. Print.

Horvath, Rosemary. "MCC Project Offers 'Passport to the Future.'" *The Daily News* [Greenville, MI] 6 Oct. 1999. Print.

Horvath, Rosemary. "MCC Wins Tech Center Grant." *The Daily News* [Greenville, MI] 28 Aug 2001. Print.

Jeltema, Ryan. "Getting Situated." *The Daily News* [Greenville, MI] Jul. 2009. Print.

Jeltema, Ryan. "Looking Back, Moving Forward." *The Daily News* [Greenville, MI] 20 Oct. 2007. Print.

Johnson, Carolyn. Letter to the author. 6 Aug. 2014. Email.

Lantz, James. Personal interview. 31 Oct. 2013.

Lantz, James. Personal interview regarding Heritage Village. 21 Jan. 2011.

Leach, Hugh. "College Movers Nearer Reality." *The Daily News* [Greenville, MI] 8 Apr. 1966. Print.

Leach, Hugh. "MCC Makes Changes in Campus Plans." *The Daily News* [Greenville, MI] 18 Jan. 1966. Print.

List, Ryon. "MCC Is Becoming More of an Asset." *The Daily News* [Greenville, MI] 31 Dec. 2005. Print.

List, Ryon. "Carbonelli Notes Need for Science Expansion." *The Daily News* [Greenville, MI] 31 Dec. 2005. Print.

List, Ryon. "MCC's Continuing Ed Director." *The Daily News* [Greenville, MI] 4 Mar. 2002. Print.

Lund, Lisa. "Review of Student Success Efforts at MCC." Montcalm Community College. 13 Oct. 2014. Print.

Mack, Samantha. "MCC Administrator Discovered Her Passion as a Student." Press release. Montcalm Community College. 2 Sep. 2014. Typescript.

Mack, Samantha. "MCC Names Buildings after College Supporters." Press release. Montcalm Community College. May 2015. Typescript.

Mahan, Mildred. Letter to the author. 13 Feb. 2011. Handwritten.

Main, Sandy. "Center of it All." *The Daily News* [Greenville, MI] 26 Dec. 2005. Print.

Marston, Bob. Letter to the author. 23 Feb. 2011. Handwritten.

Montcalm Community Chapter of Institute for Life Long Learning. "Constitution/Bylaws of Life-Long Learners." Montcalm Community College. Rev., 12 Sep. 2014. Print.

Montcalm Community College. *Catalog.* Sidney, MI: Montcalm Community College, Separate editions for years 1966 through 2014 [except 1971]. Print.

Montcalm Community College. "Created to Serve." Press release. 22 Sep. 1965. Typescript.

Montcalm Community College. *Join the Club.* Sidney, MI: Montcalm Community College, n.d. Print.

Montcalm Community College. Summary of Board of Trustee Minutes, October 1964 to June 2009. 28 Jun. 2009. Typescript.

Montcalm Community College. Trustee-O-Gram Board Minute Summaries. Sidney, MI: Montcalm Community College, 2009-2014. Typescript.

Montcalm Community College Foundation. "Making a Difference." Montcalm Community College. N.d. Print.

Morais, Sally. Personal interview. 1 Jul. 2014.

Morais, Sally. Letter to author. 22 May 2014.

Morford, Leslie. Personal interview. 7 Jun. 2012.

Mulder, Dennis. Personal interview. 9 Jun. 2014.

Odette, Dave. "Paleontologist Discusses Study of 1,000-Year-Old Mastodon Bone." *The Daily News* [Greenville, MI] 20 Nov. 1986. Print.

David Pritchard, Telephone interview. 18 Nov. 2014.

Rehmann, Marc. "Local Businesses Use M-TEC for Training." List, Ryon. *The Daily News* [Greenville, MI] 28 Dec.. 2005. Print.

Seiter, William. Personal interview. 22 Oct. 2013.

Sentinel Standard. "Ferrentino Begins as MCC's Fifth President." [Ionia, MI] 9 Jul. 2009. Print.

Shoen, Barney. Letter to the author. 19 Feb. 2011. Handwritten.

Simon, Charles W. Jr. "Final Report of the Citizens Study Council – Montcalm County Community College Study." East Lansing: MI, The Office of Community College Cooperation, Michigan State University, Max S. Smith, Director of the Study. Jun. 1964. Print.

Smith, Cory. "MCC Bill Braman Family Center for Education Opens in Greenville." [Greenville: MI] 26 Apr. 2013. Print.

Smith, Kenneth. Personal interview. 3 Jun. 2014.

Smith, Kenneth. Letter to the author. N.d. Typescript.

Smith, Terence. "Past, Present and Future: Four MCC Presidents Meet." *The Daily News* [Greenville, MI] 22 Jun. 1984. Print.

Smith, Terry. "Howard City Center." Press release. Montcalm Community College. 21 Mar. 1999. Typescript.

Smith, Terry. "M-TEC Grand Opening." Press release. Montcalm Community College. 7 Sep. 2001. Typescript.

Smith, Terry. Personal interview. 30 Jul. 2014.

Snook, Daniel. Personal interview. 6 Jun. 2014.

Springsteen, Lois. Personal interview. 22 Oct. 2014.

Springsteen, Lois. "Dr. Herbert Stoutenburg." Press release. Montcalm Community College. 23 Mar. 1978. Typescript.

Springsteen, Lois. "Keeping Posted" Sidney: MI. Montcalm Community College, N.d. Mimeographed.

Springsteen, Lois. "Montcalm Community College President Herbert N. Stoutenburg is Retiring." Press release. Montcalm Community College. 22 Jun. 1984. Typescript.

Springsteen, Lois. "Natatorium Ready for Use." Press release. Montcalm Community College. 1 Sep. 1976. Typescript.

Springsteen, Lois. "New President at Montcalm College." *Howard City Record* [Howard City, MI] 29 Mar. 1978. Print.

Stafford, John. "Timely Leadership at MCC." *The Daily News* [Greenville, MI] 26 Jun. 1984. Print.

Strautz-Springborn, Shelly. "MCC Unveils Stanley P. Ash Building, Announces Capital Campaign." Press release. Montcalm Community College. 19 Oct. 2007. Typescript.

The Daily News. "Community College Meeting December 9." [Greenville, MI] 3 Dec. 1964. Print.

The Daily News. "1 Mill Would Finance New Community College." [Greenville, MI] 22 Oct. 1964. Print.

Walker, Marcia. "Santa Visits MCC for Super Sunday." *The Daily News* [Greenville, MI] Dec. 1989. Print.

The Daily News. "College Set to Open; Dedication Sept. 26." [Greenville, MI] 24 Aug. 1967. Print.

The Daily News. "First Graduation Scheduled Friday." [Greenville, MI] 7 Jun. 1967. Print.

The Daily News. "MCC Offers Several Pool Options." [Greenville, MI] 11 Jun. 1986. Print.

The Daily News. "MCC Project Ahead of Schedule." [Greenville, MI] 10 Mar. 1999. Print.

The Daily News. "MCC Unveils New Life Science Building." [Greenville, MI] 1 Nov. 2007. Print.

Thomsen, Ilene. Letter to the author. 24 Feb. 2011. Handwritten.

Vander Mark, Valerie. Letter to the author. 7 Sep. 2014. Email.

Vander Mark, Valerie. Letter to the author. 19 May. 2015. Email.

Walker, Marcia. "MCC to Display Crystal Mastodon Bones." *The Daily News* [Greenville, MI] 13 Aug. 1986. Print.

Willison, Pat. Letter to author. 22 Oct. 2014.

Gary Hauck displays the new items placed into the MCC time capsule along with the original artifacts. The combined capsule will be opened in the year 2040 during the college's 75th anniversary.

About the Author

———•◆•◆•◆•———

D r. Gary L. Hauck served as a member of the 50th anniversary committee. He is dean of instruction and student development at the Montcalm Community College in Sidney, Michigan, where he also teaches humanities, religion, and philosophy. He holds the BRE and ThB degrees from Summit University, a ThM from Dallas Theological Seminary, and a PhD from Michigan State University, where he received the Richard L. Featherstone Award and Donald O. Tatroe Award for Scholarship.

Hauck has been a member of the Montcalm Area Art Association, Mid-Michigan Arts Council, Flat River Historical Society, Montcalm Heritage Village Committee, the BIS Advisory Board of Ferris State University, and the College Advisory Committee of the World Affairs Council of Western Michigan. He has served as a co-chair and member of the One Book One County Montcalm planning committee, and has also been on the board of the Montcalm Area Reading Council. Hauck is the founder of the Montcalm Area Humanities Council, which he served as its first chairman. He is the vice president of the Michigan Liberal Arts Deans association.

Hauck has traveled to all 50 states and 50 countries, leading student groups to many of these. He has taught college courses in China, Ecuador, and Russia, and has participated in archeological digs in the Middle East. For these reasons, he helped to establish MCC's study abroad program, and foster a more culturally- and globally-oriented environment on the college campus, directing the school's special events planning. Hauck is the author of 17 books including, *Organizational*

Transformation in Higher Education, Exploring Humanities Around the World, and *The Story of Heritage Village – Celebrating 25 Years.*

Married for 43 years to Lois Thornton (author of *The Caregiver,* and co-author with Gary of *Spiritual Formation* and *Master of Disaster, The Life and Works of Shipwreck Artist Ed Pusick*), the Haucks live in West Michigan and have four children: Heidi (& Steve), Greg (& Rachel), Andrew (& Becky), and Jared (& Rachel); and two grandchildren, Jacob and Liliana.

Printed in the United States
By Bookmasters